CONTENTS

INTRODUCTION. 9

I. ODES OF THE TEMPLE AND THE ALTAR. 33
II. THE MINOR ODES OF THE KINGDOM. 76
III. THE MAJOR ODES OF THE KINGDOM. 101
IV. LESSONS FROM THE STATES. 144

THE SHIH KING

Copyright © 2008 BiblioBazaar
All rights reserved

Original copyright: 1879

JAMES LEGGE

THE SHIH KING

OR
BOOK OF POETRY

ALL THE PIECES AND STANZAS IN IT
ILLUSTRATING THE RELIGIOUS VIEWS AND
PRACTICES OF THE WRITERS AND THEIR TIMES.

From the Sacred Books of the East, Vol. 3

THE SHIH KING

INTRODUCTION.

CHAPTER I.

THE NAME AND CONTENTS OF THE CLASSIC.

1. Among the Chinese classical books next after the Shû in point of antiquity comes the Shih or Book of Poetry.

The meaning of the character Shih.

The character Shû, as formed by the combination of two others, one of which signified 'a pencil,' and the other 'to speak,' supplied, we saw in its structure, an indication of its primary significance, and furnished a clue to its different applications. The character Shih was made on a different principle, that of phonetical formation, in the peculiar sense of these words when applied to a large class of Chinese terms. The significative portion of it is the character for 'speech,' but the other half is merely phonetical, enabling us to approximate to its pronunciation or name. The meaning of the compound has to be learned from its usage. Its most common significations are 'poetry,' 'a poem, or poems,' and a collection of poems! This last is its meaning when we speak of the Shih or the Shih King.

The earliest Chinese utterance that we have on the subject of poetry is that in the Shû by the ancient Shun, when he said to his Minister of Music, 'Poetry is the Expression of earnest thought, and singing is the prolonged utterance of that expression.' To the

9

same effect is the language of a Preface to the Shih, sometimes ascribed to Confucius and certainly older than our Christian era: 'Poetry is the product of earnest thought. Thought cherished in the mind becomes earnest; then expressed in words, it becomes poetry. The feelings move inwardly, and are embodied in words. When words are insufficient for them, recourse is had to sighs and exclamations. When sighs and exclamations are insufficient for them, recourse is had to the prolonged utterance of song. When this again is insufficient, unconsciously the hands begin to move and the feet to dance . . . To set forth correctly the successes and failures (of government), to affect Heaven and Earth, and to move spiritual beings, there is no readier instrument than poetry.'

Rhyme, it may be added here, is a necessary accompaniment of poetry in the estimation of the Chinese. Only in a very few pieces of the Shih is it neglected.

The contents of the Shih.

2. The Shih King contains 305 Pieces and the titles of six others. The most recent of them are assigned to the reign of king Ting of the Kâu dynasty, B.C. 606 to 586, and the oldest, forming a group of only five, to the period of the Shang dynasty which preceded that of Kâu, B.C. 1766 to 1123. Of those five, the latest piece should be referred to the twelfth century B.C., and the most ancient may have been composed five centuries earlier. All the other pieces in the Shih have to be distributed over the time between Ting and king Wan, the founder of the line of Kâu. The distribution, however, is not equal nor continuous. There were some reigns of which we do not have a single Poetical fragment.

The whole collection is divided into four parts, called the Kwo Fang, the Hsiâo Yâ, the Tâ Yâ, and the Sung.

The Kwo Fang, in fifteen Books, contains 160 pieces, nearly all of them short, and descriptive of manners and events in several of the feudal states of Kâu. The title has been translated by The Manners of the Different States, 'Les Mœurs des Royaumes,' and, which I prefer, by Lessons from the States.

The Hsiâo Yâ, or Lesser Yâ, in eight Books, contains seventy-four pieces and the titles of six others, sung at gatherings of the feudal princes, and their appearances at the royal court. They were produced in the royal territory, and are descriptive of the manners and ways of the government in successive reigns. It is difficult to find an English word that shall fitly represent the Chinese Yâ as here used. In his Latin translation of the Shih, p. Lacharme translated Hsiâo Yâ by 'Quod rectum est, sed inferiore ordine,' adding in a note:—'Siâo Yâ, latine Parvum Rectum, quia in hac Parte mores describuntur, recti illi quidem, qui tamen nonnihil a recto deflectunt.' But the manners described are not less correct or incorrect, as the case may be, than those of the states in the former Part or of the kingdom in the next. I prefer to call this Part 'Minor Odes of the Kingdom,' without attempting to translate the term Yâ.

The Tâ Yâ or Greater Yâ, in three Books, contains thirty-one pieces, sung on great occasions at the royal court and in the presence of the king. p. Lacharme called it 'Magnum Rectum (Quod rectum est superiore ordine).' But there is the same objection here to the use of the word 'correct' as in the case of the pieces of the previous Part. I use the name 'Major Odes of the Kingdom.' The greater length and dignity of most of the pieces justify the distinction of the two Parts into Minor and Major.

The Sung, also in three Books, contains forty pieces, thirty-one of which belong to the sacrificial services at the royal court of Kâu; four, to those of the marquises of Lû; and five to the corresponding sacrifices of the kings of Shang. p. Lacharme denominated them correctly 'Parentales Cantus.' In the Preface to the Shih, to which I have made reference above, it is said, 'The Sung are pieces in admiration of the embodied manifestation of complete virtue, announcing to the spiritual Intelligences their achievement thereof.' Kû Hsî's account of the Sung was—'Songs for the Music of the Ancestral Temple;' and that of Kiang Yung of the present dynasty—'Songs for the Music at Sacrifices.' I have united these two definitions, and call the Part—'Odes of the Temple and the Altar.' There is a difference between the pieces of Lû and the other two collections in this Part, to which I will call attention in giving the translation of them.

Only the pieces of the fourth Part have professedly a religious character.

From the above account of the contents of the Shih, it will be seen that only the pieces in the last of its four Parts are professedly of a religious character. Many of those, however, in the other Parts, especially the second and third, describe religious services, and give expression to religious ideas in the minds of their authors.

Classification of the pieces from their form and style.

3. Some of the pieces in the Shih are ballads, some are songs, some are hymns, and of others the nature can hardly be indicated by any English denomination They have often been spoken of by the general name of odes, understanding by that term lyric poems that were set to music.

My reason for touching here on this point is the earliest account of the Shih, as a collection either already formed or in the process of formation, that we find in Chinese literature. In the Official Book of Kâu, generally supposed to be a work of the twelfth or eleventh century B.C., among the duties of the Grand Music-Master there is 'the teaching,' (that is, to the musical performers,) 'the, six classes of poems:—the Fang; the Fû; the Pî; the Hsing; the Yâ; and the Sung.' That the collection of the Shih, as it now is, existed so early as the date assigned to the Official Book could not be; but we find the same account of it given in the so-called Confucian Preface. The Fang, the Yâ, and the Sung are the four Parts of the classic described in the preceding paragraph, the Yâ embracing both the Minor and Major Odes of the Kingdom. But what were the Fû, the Pî, and the Hsing? We might suppose that they were the names of three other distinct Parts or Books. But they were not so. Pieces so discriminated are found in all the four Parts, though there are more of them in the first two than in the others.

The Fû may be described as Narrative pieces, in which the writers tell what they have to say in a simple, straightforward manner, without any hidden meaning reserved in the mind. The metaphor and other figures of speech enter into their composition as freely as in descriptive poems in any other language.

The Pî are Metaphorical pieces, in which the poet has under his language a different meaning from what it expresses,—a meaning which there should be nothing in that language to indicate. Such a piece may be compared to the Æsopic fable; but, while it is the object of the fable to inculcate the virtues of morality and prudence, an historical interpretation has to be sought for the metaphorical pieces of the Shih. Generally, moreover, the moral of the fable is subjoined to it, which is never done. in the case of these pieces.

The Hsing have been called Allusive pieces. They are very remarkable, and more numerous than the metaphorical. They often commence with a couple of lines which are repeated without change, or with slight rhythmical changes, in all the stanzas. In other pieces different stanzas have allusive lines peculiar to themselves. Those lines are descriptive, for the most part, of some object or circumstance in the animal or vegetable world, and after them the poet proceeds to his proper subject. Generally, the allusive lines convey a meaning harmonizing with those which follow, where an English poet would begin the verses with Like or As. They are really metaphorical, but the difference between an allusive and a metaphorical piece is this,— that in the former the writer proceeds to state the theme which his mind is occupied with, while no such intimation is given in the latter. Occasionally, it is difficult,. not to say impossible, to discover the metaphorical idea in the allusive lines, and then we can only deal with them as a sort of refrain.

In leaving this subject, it is only necessary to say further that the allusive, the metaphorical, and the narrative elements sometimes all occur in the same piece.

CHAPTER II.

THE SHIH BEFORE CONFUCIUS, AND WHAT, IF ANY, WERE HIS LABOURS UPON IT.

Statement of Sze-mâ Khien.

1. Sze-mâ Khien, in his memoir of Confucius, says. 'The old poems amounted to more than 3000. Confucius removed

those which were only repetitions of others, and selected those which would be serviceable for the inculcation of propriety and righteousness. Ascending as high as Hsieh and Hâu-kî, and descending through the prosperous eras of Yin and Kâu to the times of decadence under kings Yû and Lî, he selected in all 305 pieces, which he' sang over to his lute, to bring them into accordance with the musical style of the Shâo, the Wû, the Yâ, and the Fang.'

The writer of the Records of the Sui Dynasty.

In the History of the Classical Books in the Records of the Sui Dynasty (A.D.589 to 618), it is said:—'When royal benign rule ceased, and poems were no more collected, Kih, the Grand Music-Master of Lû, arranged in order those that were existing, and made a copy of them. Then Confucius expurgated them; and going up to the Shang dynasty, and coming down to the state of Lû, he compiled altogether 300 Pieces.'

Opinion of Kû Hsî.

Kû Hsî, whose own standard work on the Shih appeared in A.D. 1178, declined to express himself positively on the expurgation of the odes, but summed up his view of what Confucius did for them in the following words:—'Royal methods had ceased, and poems were no more collected. Those which were extant were full of errors, and wanting in arrangement. When Confucius returned from Wei to Lû, he brought with him the odes that he had gotten in other states, and digested them, along with those that were to be found in Lû, into a collection Of 300 pieces.'

View of the author.

I have not been able to find evidence sustaining these representations, and must adopt the view that, before the birth of Confucius, the Book of Poetry existed, substantially the same as it was at his death, and that while he may have somewhat altered the arrangement of its Books and pieces, the service which he rendered to it was not that of compilation, but the impulse to study it which he communicated to his disciples.

Groundlessness of Khien's statement.

2. If we place Khien's composition of the memoir of Confucius in B.C. 100, nearly four hundred years will have elapsed between the death of the sage and any statement to the effect that he expurgated previously existing poems, or compiled the collection that we now have; and no writer in the interval affirmed or implied any such things. The further statement in the Sui Records about the Music-Master of Lû is also without any earlier confirmation. But independently of these considerations, there is ample evidence to prove, first, that the poems current before Confucius were not by any means so numerous as Khien says, and, secondly, that the collection of 300 pieces or thereabouts, digested under the same divisions as in the present classic, existed before the sage's time.

3. i. It would not be surprising, if floating about and current among the people of China in the sixth century before our era, there had been more than 3000 pieces of poetry. The marvel is that such was not the case. But in the Narratives of the States, a work of the Kâu dynasty, and ascribed by many to Zo Khiû-ming, there occur quotations from thirty-one poems, made by statesmen and others, all anterior to Confucius; and of those poems there are not more than two which are not in the present classic. Even of those two, one is an ode of it quoted under another name. Further, in the Zo Kwan, certainly the work of Khiû-ming, we have quotations from not fewer than 219 poems, of which only thirteen are not found in the classic. Thus of 250 poems current in China before the supposed compilation of the Shih, 236 are found in it, and only fourteen are absent. To use the words of Kâu Yî, a scholar of the present dynasty, 'If the poems existing in Confucius' time had been more than 3000, the quotations of poems now lost in these two works should have been ten times as numerous as the quotations from the 305 pieces said to have been preserved by him, whereas they are only between a twenty-first and twenty-second part of the existing pieces. This is sufficient to show that Khien's statement is not worthy of credit.'

ii. Of the existence of the Book of Poetry before Confucius, digested in four Parts, and much in the same order as at present, there may be advanced the following proofs:—

First. There is the passage in the Official Book of Kâu, quoted and discussed in the last paragraph of the preceding chapter. We have in it a distinct reference to poems, many centuries before the sage, arranged and classified in the same way as those of the existing Shih. Our Shih, no doubt, was then in the process of formation.

Second. Lî the ninth piece of the sixth decade of the Shih, Part II, an ode assigned to the time of king Yû, B.C. 78, to 771, we have the words,

> 'They sing the Yâ and the Nan,
> Dancing to their flutes without error.'

So early, therefore, as the eighth century B.C. there was a collection of poems, of which some bore the name of the Nan, which there is much reason to suppose were the Kâu Nan and the Shâo Nan, forming the first two Books of the first Part of the present Shih; and of which others bore the name of the Yâ, being, probably, the earlier pieces that now compose a large portion of the second and third Parts.

Third. In the narratives of Zo Khiû-ming, under the twenty-ninth year of duke Hsiang, B.C. 544, when Confucius was only seven or eight years old, we have an account of a visit to the court of Lû by an envoy from Wû, an eminent statesman of the time, and a man of great learning. We are told that as he wished to hear the music of Kâu, which he could do better in Lû than in any other state, they sang to him the odes of the Kâu Nan and the Shâo Nan; those of Phei, Yung, and Wei; of the Royal Domain; of Kang; of Khî; of Pin; of Khin; of Wei; of Thang; of Khan; of Kwei; and of Zhâo. They sang to him also the odes of the Minor Yâ and the Greater Yâ; and they sang finally the pieces of the Sung. We have thus, existing in the boyhood of Confucius, what we may call the present Book of Poetry, with its Fang, its Yâ, and its Sung. The only difference discernible is slight,-in the order in which the Books of the Fang followed one another.

Fourth. We may appeal in this matter to the words of Confucius himself. Twice in the Analects he speaks of the Shih as a collection consisting of 300 pieces[1]. That work not being made on any principle of chronological order, we cannot positively assign those sayings to any particular years of Confucius' life; but it is, I may say, the unanimous opinion of Chinese critics that they were spoken before the time to which Khien and Kû Hsî refer his special labour on the Book of Poetry.

To my own mind the evidence that has been adduced is decisive on the points which I specified. The Shih, arranged very much as we now have it, was current in China before the time of Confucius, and its pieces were in the mouths of statesmen and scholars, constantly quoted by them on festive and other occasions. Poems not included in it there doubtless were, but they were comparatively few. Confucius may have made a copy for the use of himself and his disciples; but it does not appear that he rejected any pieces which had been previously received into the collection, or admitted any which had not previously found a place in it.

What Confucius did for the Shih.

4. The question now arises of what Confucius did for the Shih, if, indeed, he did anything at all. The only thing from which we can hazard an opinion on the point we have from himself. In the Analects, IX, xiv, he tells us:—'I returned from Wei to Lû, and then the music was reformed, and the pieces in

1. In stating that the odes were 300, Confucius probably preferred to use the round number. There are, as I said in the 'former chapter, altogether 305 pieces, which is the number given by Sze-mâ Khien. There are also the titles of six others. It is contended by Kû Hsî and many other scholars that these titles were only the names of tunes. More likely is the view that the text of the pieces so styled was lost after Confucius' death.

the Yâ and the Sung received their proper places.' The return from Wei to Lû took place only five years before the sage's death. He ceased from that time to take an active part in political affairs, and solaced himself with music, the study of the ancient literature of his nation, the writing of 'the Spring and Autumn,' and familiar intercourse with those of his disciples who still kept around him. He reformed the music,—that to which the pieces of the Shih were sung; but wherein the reformation consisted we cannot tell. And he gave to the pieces of the Yâ and the Sung their proper places. The present order of the Books in the Fang, slightly differing from what was common in his boyhood, may have now been determined by him. More than this we cannot say

While we cannot discover, therefore, any peculiar and important labours of Confucius on the Shih, and we have it now, as will be shown in the next chapter, substantially as he found it already compiled to his hand, the subsequent preservation of it may reasonably be attributed to the admiration which he expressed for it, and the enthusiasm for it with which he sought to inspire his disciples. It was one of the themes on which he delighted to converse with them[1]. He taught that it is from the poems that the mind receives its best stimulus[2]. A man ignorant of them was, in his opinion, like one who stands with his face towards a wall, limited in his view, and unable to advance [3]. Of the two things that his son could specify as enjoined on him by the sage, the first was that he should learn the odes[4]. In this way Confucius, probably, contributed largely to the subsequent preservation of the Shih, the preservation of the tablets on which the odes were inscribed, and the preservation of it in the memory of all who venerated his authority, and looked up to him as their master.

1. Analects, VII, xvii.
2 Analects, VIII, viii, XVII, ix.
3. Analects, XVII, x.
4. Analects, XVI, xiii.

CHAPTER III.

THE SHIH FROM THE TIME OF CONFUCIUS TILL THE GENERAL ACKNOWLEDGMENT OF THE PRESENT TEXT.

From Confucius to rise of the Khin dynasty.

1. Of the attention paid to the study of the Shih from the death of Confucius to the rise -of the Khin dynasty, we have abundant evidence in the writings of his the grandson Dze-sze, of Mencius,

and of Hsün Khing. One of the acknowledged distinctions of Mencius is his acquaintance with the odes, his quotations from which are very numerous; and Hsün Khing survived the extinction of the Kâu dynasty, and lived on into the times of Khin.

The Shih was all recovered, after the fires of Khin.

2. The Shih shared in the calamity which all the other classical works, excepting the Yî, suffered, when the tyrant of Khin issued his edict for their destruction. But I have shown, in the Introduction to the Shû, p. 7, that that edict was in force for less than a quarter of a century. The odes were all, or very nearly all[1], recovered; and the reason assigned for this is, that their preservation depended on the memory of scholars more than on their inscription on tablets of bamboo and on silk.

Three different texts.

3. Three different texts of the Shih made their appearance early in the Han dynasty, known as the Shih of Lû, of Khî, and of Han; that is, the Book of Poetry was recovered from three different quarters. Liû Hin's Catalogue of the Books in the Imperial Library of Han (B.C. 6 to 1) commences, on the Shih King, with a collection of the three texts, in twenty-eight chapters.

1. All, in fact, unless we except the six pieces of Part II, of which we have only the titles. It is contended by Kû Hsî and others that the text of these had been lost before the time of Confucius. It may have been lost, however, after the sage's death; see note on p. 283.

The text of Lû.

1. Immediately after the mention of the general collection in the Catalogue come the titles of two works of commentary on the text of Lû. The former of them was by a Shan Phei of whom we have some account in the Literary Biographies of Han. He was a native of Lû, and had received his own knowledge of the odes from a scholar of Khî, called Fâu Khiû-po. He was resorted to by many disciples, whom he taught to repeat the odes. When the first emperor of the Han dynasty was passing through Lû, Shan followed

him to the capital of that state, and had an interview with him. Subsequently the emperor Wû (B.C. 140 to 87), in the beginning of his reign, sent for him to court when he was more than eighty years old; and he appears to have survived a considerable number of years beyond that advanced age. The names of ten of his disciples are given, all of them men of eminence, and among them Khung An-kwo. Rather later, the, most noted adherent of the school of Lû was Wei Hsien, who arrived at the dignity of prime minister (from B.C. 71 to 67), and published the Shih of Lû in Stanzas and Lines. Up and down in the Books of Han and Wei are to be found quotations of the odes, that must have been taken from the professors of the Lû recension; but neither the text nor the writings on it long survived. They are said to have perished during the Kin dynasty (A.D.265 to 419). When the Catalogue of the Sui Library was made, none of them were existing.

The text of Khî.

ii. The Han Catalogue mentions five different works on the Shih of Khî. This text was from a Yüan Kû, a native of Khî, about whom we learn, from the same collection of Literary Biographies, that he was one of the great scholars of the court in the time of the emperor King (B.C. 156 to 141),—a favourite with him, and specially distinguished for his knowledge of the odes and his advocacy of orthodox Confucian doctrine. He died in the succeeding reign of Wû, more than ninety years old; and we are told that all the scholars of Khî who got a name in those days for their acquaintance with the Shih sprang from his school. Among his disciple's was the well-known name of Hsiâ-hâu Shih-khang, who communicated his acquisitions to Hâu Zhang, a native of the present Shan-tung province, and author of two of the works in the Han Catalogue. Hâu had three disciples of note, and by them the Shih of Khî was transmitted to others, whose names, with quotations from their writings, are scattered through the Books of Han. Neither text nor commentaries, however, had a better fate than the Shih of Lû. There is no mention of them in the Catalogue of Sui. They are said to have perished even before the rise of the Kin dynasty.

The text of Han Ying.

iii. The text of Han was somewhat more fortunate. Hin's Catalogue contains the names of four works, all by Han Ying, whose surname is thus perpetuated in the text of the Shih that emanated from him. He was a native, we are told, of Yen, and a great scholar in the time of the emperor Wan (B.C. 179 to 155), and on into the reigns of King, and Wû. 'He laboured,' it is said, 'to unfold the meaning of the odes, and published an Explanation of the Text., and Illustrations of the Poems, containing several myriads of characters. His text was somewhat different from the texts of Lû and Khî, but substantially of the same meaning.' Of course, Han founded a school; but while almost all the writings of his followers soon perished, both the works just mentioned continued on through the various dynasties to the time of Sung. The Sui Catalogue contains the titles of his Text and two works on it; the Thang, those of his Text and his Illustrations; but when we come to the Catalogue of Sung, published under the Yüan dynasty, we find only the Illustrations, in ten books or chapters; and Âu-yang Hsiû (A.D. 1017 to 1072) tells us that in his time this was all of Han that remained. It continues entire, or nearly so, to the present day.

A fourth text; that of Mâo.

4. But while those three different recensions of the Shih all disappeared, with the exception of a single treatise of Han Ying, their unhappy fate was owing not more to the convulsions by which the empire was often rent, and the consequent destruction of literary monuments such as we have witnessed in China in our own day, than to the appearance of a fourth text, which displaced them by its superior correctness, and the ability with which it was advocated and commented on. This was what is called the Text of Mâo. It came into the field rather later than the others; but the Han Catalogue contains the Shih of Mâo, in twenty-nine chapters, and a Commentary on it in thirty-nine. According to Kang Hsüan, the author of this was a native of Lû, known as Mâo Hang or 'the Greater Mâo,' who had been a disciple, we are told by Lü Tch-ming, of Hsün Khing. The work is lost. He had communicated his knowledge of the Shih, however, to

another Mâo,—Mâo Kang, 'the Lesser Mao,' who was a great scholar, at the court of king Hsien of Ho-kien, a son of the emperor King. King Hsien was one of the most diligent labourers in the recovery of the ancient books, and presented the text and work of Hang at the court of his father,—probably in B.C. 129. Mâo Kang published Explanations of the Shih, in twenty-nine chapters,—a work which we still possess; but it was not till the reign of Phing (A.D. 1 to 9) that Mâo's recension was received into the Imperial College, and took its place along with those of Lû, Khî, and Han Ying.

The Chinese critics nave carefully traced the line of scholars who had charge of Mâo's Text and Explanations down to the reign of Phing. The names of the men and their works are all given. By the end of the first quarter of our first century we find the most famous scholars addicting themselves to Mâo's text. The well-known Kiâ Khwei (A.D. 30 to 101) published a work on the Meaning and Difficulties of Mâo's Shih, having previously compiled a digest of the differences between its text and those of the other three recensions, at the command of the emperor Ming (A.D. 58 to 75). The equally celebrated Mâ Yung (A.D. 79 to 166) followed with another commentary;—and we arrive at Kang Hsüan or Kang Khang-khang (A.D. 127 to 200), who wrote a Supplementary Commentary to the Shih of Mâo, and a Chronological Introduction to the Shih. The former of these two works complete, and portions of the latter, are still extant. After the time of King the other three texts were little heard of, while the name of the commentators on Mâo's text speedily becomes legion. It was inscribed, moreover, on the stone tablets of the emperor Ling (A.D. 168 to 189). The grave of Mâo Kang is still shown near the village of Zun-fû, in the departmental district of Ho-kien, Kih-lî.

The different texts guarantee the genuineness of the recovered Shih.

5. Returning now to what I said in the second paragraph, it will be granted that the appearance of three different and independent texts, soon after the rise of the Ha dynasty, affords the most satisfactory a evidence of the recovery of the Book of Poetry as it had continued from the time of Confucius. Unfortunately, only fragments of those texts remain now; but they were, while they were current, diligently compared with one another, and with the

fourth text of Mâo, which subsequently got the field to itself. When a collection is made of their peculiar readings, so far as it can now be done, it is clear that their variations from one another and from Mâo's text arose from the alleged fact that the preservation of the odes was owing to their being transmitted by recitation. The rhyme helped the memory to retain them, and while wood, bamboo, and silk had all been consumed by the flames of Khin, when the time of repression ceased, scholars would be eager to rehearse their stores. It was inevitable, and more so in China than in a country possessing an alphabet, that the same sounds when taken down by different writers should be represented by different characters.

On the whole, the evidence given above is as full as could be desired in such a case, and leaves no reason for us to hesitate in accepting the present received text of the Shih as a very close approximation to that which was current in the time of Confucius.

CHAPTER IV.

THE FORMATION OF THE COLLECTION OF THE SHIH HOW IT CAME TO BE SO SMALL AND INCOMPLETE; THE INTERPRETATION AND AUTHORS OF THE PIECES; ONE POINT OF TIME CERTAINLY INDICATED IN IT; AND THE CONFUCIAN PREFACE.

1. It has been shown above, in the second chapter, that the Shih existed as a collection of poetical pieces before the time of Confucius[1]. In order to complete this Introduction to it, it is desirable to give some account of the various subjects indicated in the heading of the present chapter.

How were the odes collected in the first place? In his Account of a Conversation concerning 'a Right Regulation of Governments for the Common Good of Mankind' (Edinburgh, 1704), p. 10, Sir Andrew Fletcher, of Saltoun, tells us the opinion of 'a very wise man,' that 'if a man were permitted to make all the ballads of a nation, he need not care who should make its laws.' A writer in the Spectator, no. 502, refers to a similar opinion as having been entertained in England earlier than the time of Fletcher. 'I have heard,' he says, 'that a minister of state in the reign of Elizabeth had all manner of books and ballads brought to him, of what kind soever, and took great notice how they took with the people; upon which he would, and certainly might, very well judge of their present dispositions, and of the most proper way of applying them according to his own purposes [2].'

1. As in the case of the Shû, Confucius generally speaks of 'the Shih,' never using the name of 'the Shih King.' In the Analects, IX, xiv, however, he mentions also the Yâ and the Sung; and in XVII, x, he specifies the Kâu Nan and the Shâo Nan, the first two books of the Kwo Fang. Mencius similarly speaks of 'the Shih;' and in III, i, ch. 4, he specifies 'the Sung of Lû,' Book ii of Part IV. In VI, ii, ch. 3, he gives his views of the Hsiâo Phan, the third ode of decade 5, Part II, and of the Khâi Fung, the seventh ode of Book iii of Part I.
2 This passage from the Spectator is adduced by Sir John Davis in his treatise on the Poetry of the Chinese, p. 35.

The theory of the Chinese scholars about a collection of poems for governmental purposes.

In harmony with the views thus expressed is the theory of the Chinese scholars, that it was the duty of the ancient kings to make themselves acquainted with all the poems current in the different states, and to judge from them of the rule exercised by the several princes, so that they might minister praise or blame, reward or punishment accordingly.

The rudiments of this theory may be found in the Shû, in the Canon of Shun; but the one classical passage which is appealed to in support of it is in the Record of Rites, III, ii, parr. 13, 14:—'Every fifth year, the Son of Heaven made a progress through the kingdom, when the Grand Music-Master was commanded to lay before him the poems of the different states, as an exhibition of the manners and government of the people.' Unfortunately, this Book of the Lî Kî, the

Royal Ordinances, was compiled only in the reign of the emperor Wan of the Han dynasty (B.C. 179 to 155). The scholars entrusted with the work did their best, we may suppose, with the materials at their command they made much use, it is evident, of Mencius, and of the Î Lî. The Kâu Lî, or the Official Book of Kâu, had not then been recovered. But neither in Mencius nor in the Î Lî do we meet with any authority for the statement before us. The Shû mentions that Shun every fifth year made a tour of inspection; but there were then no odes for him to examine, for to him and his minister Kâo-yâo is attributed the first rudimentary attempt at the poetic art. Of the progresses of the Hsiâ and Yin sovereigns we have no information; and those of the kings Of Kâu were made, we know, only once in twelve years. The statement in the Royal Ordinances, therefore, was probably based only on tradition.

Notwithstanding the difficulties that beset this passage of the Li Kî, I am not disposed to reject it altogether. It derives a certain amount of confirmation from the passage quoted from the Official Book of Kâu on p. 278, showing that in the Kâu dynasty there was a collection of poems, under the divisions of the Fang, the Yâ, and the Sung, which it was the business of the Grand, Music-Master to teach the musicians of the court. It may be accepted then, that the duke of Kâu, in legislating for his dynasty, enacted that the poems produced in the different feudal states should be collected on occasion of the royal progresses, and lodged thereafter among the archives of the bureau of music at the royal court. The same thing, we may presume à fortiori, would be done, at certain other stated times, with those produced within the royal domain itself.

The music-master of the king would get the odes of each state from its music-master.

But the feudal states were modelled after the pattern of the royal state. They also had their music-masters, their musicians, and their historiographers. The kings in their progresses did not visit each particular state, so that the Grand Music Master could have the opportunity to collect the odes in it for himself. They met, at well-known points, the marquises, earls, barons, &c., of the different quarters of the kingdom; there gave audience to them; adjudicated on their merits, and issued to them their orders. We are obliged to suppose that the princes were attended to the places of rendezvous by their music-masters, carrying with them the poetical compositions gathered in their several regions, to present them to their superior of the royal court. We can understand how, by means of the above arrangement, the poems of the whole kingdom were accumulated and arranged among the archives of the capital.

How the collected poems were disseminated through the states.

Was there any provision for disseminating thence the poems of one state among all the others? There is sufficient evidence that such dissemination was effected out in some way. Throughout the Narratives of the States, and the details of Zo Khiû-ming on the history of the Spring and Autumn, the officers of the states generally are presented to us as familiar not only with the odes of their particular states, but with those of other states as well. They appear equally well acquainted with all the Parts and Books of our present Shih; and we saw how the whole of it was sung over to Kî Kâ of Wû, when he visited the court of Lû in the boyhood of Confucius. There was, probably, a regular communication from the royal court to the courts of the various states of the poetical pieces that for one reason or another were thought worthy of preservation. This is nowhere expressly stated, but it may be contended for by analogy from the accounts which I have given, in the Introduction to the Shû, pp. 4, 5, of the duties of the royal historiographers or recorders.

How the Shih is so small and incomplete.

2. But if the poems produced in the different states were thus collected in the capital, and thence again disseminated throughout the kingdom, we might conclude that the collection would have been far more extensive and complete than we have it now. The smallness of it is to be accounted for by the disorder into which the kingdom fell after the lapse of a few reigns from king Wû. Royal progresses ceased when royal government fell into decay, and then the odes were no more collected[1]. We have no account of any progress of the kings during the Khun Khiû period. But before that period there is a long gap of nearly 150 years between kings Khang

and Î, covering the reigns of Khang, Kâo, Mû, and Kung, if we except two doubtful pieces among the Sacrificial Odes of Kâu. The reign of Hsiâo, who succeeded to Î, is similarly uncommemorated; and the latest odes are of the time of Ting, when 100 years of the Khun Khiû period had still to run their course. Many odes must have been made and collected during the 140 and more years after king Khang. The probability is that they perished during the feeble reigns of Î and the three monarchs who followed him. Then came the long and vigorous reign of Hsüan (B.C. 827 to 782), when we may suppose that the ancient custom of collecting the poems was revived. After him all was in the main decadence and confusion. It was probably in the latter part of his reign that King-khâo, an ancestor of Confucius, obtained from the Grand Music-Master at the court of Kâu twelve of the sacrificial odes of the previous dynasty, as will be related under the Sacrificial Odes of Shang, with which he returned to Sung,

1. See Mencius, IV, ii, ch. 21.

which was held by representatives of the line of Shang. They were used there in sacrificing to the old Shang kings; yet seven of the twelve were lost before the time of the sage.

The general conclusion to which we come is, that the existing Shih is the fragment of various collections made during the early reigns of the kings of Kâu, and added to at intervals, especially on the occurrence of a prosperous rule, in accordance with the regulation that has been preserved in the Lî Kî. How it is that we have in Part I odes of comparatively few of the states into which the kingdom was divided, and that the odes of those states extend only over a short period of their history:—for these things we cannot account further than by saying that such were the ravages of time and the results of disorder. We can only accept the collection as it is, and be thankful for it. How long before Confucius the collection was closed we cannot tell.

Bearing of these views on the interpretation of particular pieces.

3. The conclusions which I have thus sought to establish concerning the formation of the Shih as a collection have an

important bearing on the interpretation of many of the pieces. The remark of Sze-mâ Khien that Confucius selected those pieces which would be service able for the inculcation of propriety and righteousness' is as erroneous as the other, that be selected 305 pieces out of more than 3000. The sage merely studied and taught the pieces which he found existing, and the collection necessarily contained odes illustrative of bad government as well as of good, of licentiousness as well as of a pure morality. Nothing has been such a stumbling-block in the way of the reception of Kû Hsî's interpretation of the pieces as the readiness with which he attributes a licentious meaning to many of those in the seventh Book of Part I. But the reason why the kings had the odes of the different states collected and presented to them was, 'that they might judge from them of the manners of the people,' and so come to a decision regarding the government and morals of their rulers. A student and translator of the odes has simply to allow them to speak for themselves, and has no more reason to be surprised by references to vice in some of them than by the language of virtue in many others. Confucius said, indeed, in his own enigmatical way, that the single sentence, 'Thought without depravity,' covered the whole 300 pieces[1]; and it may very well be allowed that they were collected and preserved for the promotion of good government and virtuous manners. The merit attaching to them is that they give us faithful pictures of what was good and what was bad in the political state of the country, and in the social, moral, and religious habits of the people.

The writers of the odes.

The pieces were of course made by individuals who possessed the gift, or thought that they possessed the gift, of poetical composition. Who they were we could tell only on the authority of the pieces themselves, or of credible historical accounts, contemporaneous with them or nearly so. It is not worth our while to question the opinion of the Chinese critics who attribute very many of them to the duke of Kâu, to whom we owe so much of the fifth Part of the Shû). There is, however, independent testimony only to his composition of a single ode,—the second of the fifteenth Book in Part I [2]. Some of the other pieces in that

Part, of which the historical interpretation may be considered as sufficiently fixed, are written in the first person; but the author may be personating his subject.

In Part II, the seventh ode of decade 2 was made by a, Kiâ-fû, a noble of the royal court, but we know nothing more about him; the sixth of decade 6, by a eunuch styled Mang-Dze; and the sixth of decade 7, from a concurrence of external testimonies, should be ascribed to duke Wû of Wei, B.C. 812 to 758.

In the third decade of Part III, the second piece was composed by the same duke Wû; the third by an earl of Zui in the royal domain; the fourth must have been made by one of king, Hsüan's ministers, to express the king's

1. Analects, II, ii.
2. See the Shû, V, vi, par. 3.

feelings under the drought that was exhausting the kingdom; and the fifth and sixth claim to be the work of Yin Kî-fû, one of Hsüan's principal officers.

4. The ninth ode of the fourth Book, Part II, gives us a note of time that enables us to fix the year of its composition in a manner entirely satisfactory, and proves also the correctness, back to that date, of the ordinary Chinese chronology. The piece is one of a group which their contents lead us to refer to the reign of king Yû, the son of Hsüan, B.C. 781 to 771. When we examine the chronology of his period, it is said that in his sixth year, B.C. 776, there was an eclipse of the sun. Now the ode commences:—

'At the conjunction (of the sun and moon) in the tenth month, on the first day of the moon, which was Hsin-mâo, the sun was eclipsed.'

This eclipse is verified by calculation as having taken place in B.C. 776, on August 29th, the very day and month assigned to it in the poem.

The Preface to the Shih.

5. In the Preface which appeared along with Mâo's text of the Shih, the occasion and authorship of many of the odes are given; but I do not allow much weight to its testimony. It is now divided

into the Great Preface and the Little Preface; but Mâo himself made no such distinction between its parts. It will be sufficient for me to give a condensed account of the views of Kû Hsî on the subject:—

'Opinions of scholars are much divided as to the authorship of the Preface. Some ascribe it to Confucius; some to (his disciple) Dze-hsiâ, and some to the historiographers of the states. In the absence of clear testimony it is impossible to decide the point, but the notice about Wei Hung (first century) in the Literary Biographies of Han[1] would seem to make it clear that the Preface was

1. The account is this: 'Hung became the disciple of Hsieh Man-khing, who was famous for his knowledge of Mâo's Shih; and he afterwards made the Preface to it, remarkable for the accuracy with which it gives the meaning of the pieces in the Fang and the Yâ, and which is now current in the world.'

his work. We must take into account, however, on the other hand, the statement of King Khang-khang, that the Preface existed as a separate document when Mâo appeared with his text, and that he broke it up, prefixing to each ode the portion belonging to it, The natural conclusion is, that the Preface had come down from a remote period, and that Hung merely added to it, and rounded it off. In accordance with this, scholars generally bold that the first sentences in the introductory notices formed the original Preface, which Mâo distributed, and that the following portions were subsequently added.

'This view may appear reasonable; but when we examine those first sentences themselves, we find that some of them do not agree with the obvious meaning of the odes to which they are prefixed, and give only rash and baseless expositions. Evidently, from the first, the Preface was made up of private speculations and conjectures on the subject-matter of the odes, and constituted a document by itself, separately appended to the text. Then on its first appearance there were current the explanations of the odes that were given in connexion with the texts of Lû, Khî, and Han Ying, so that readers could know that it was the work of later hands, and not give entire credit to it. But when Mâo no longer published the Preface as a separate document, but each ode appeared with the introductory notice as a portion of the text, this seemed to give it the authority of the text itself. Then after the other texts disappeared and Mâo's had the field to itself, this means of testing the accuracy of its prefatory notices no longer existed. They appeared as if they were the production of the poets themselves, and the odes seemed to be made from them as so many themes. Scholars handed down a faith in them from one to another, and no one ventured to express a doubt of their authority. The text was twisted and chiseled to bring it into accordance with them, and no one would undertake to say plainly that they were the work of the scholars of the Han dynasty.'

There is no western sinologist, I apprehend, who will not cordially concur with me in the principle of Kû Hsî that we must find the meaning of the poems in the poems themselves, instead of accepting the interpretation of them given by we know not whom, and to follow which would reduce many of them to absurd enigmas.

I.

ODES OF THE TEMPLE AND THE ALTAR.

IT was stated in the Introduction, p. 278, that the poems in the fourth Part of the Shih are the only ones that are professedly religious; and there are some even of them, it will be seen, which have little claim on internal grounds to be so considered.

I commence with them my selections from the Shih for the Sacred Books of the Religions of the East. I will give them all, excepting the first two of the Praise Odes of Lû, the reason for omitting which will be found. when I come to that division of the Part.

The ancestral worship of the common people.

The Odes of the Temple and the Altar are, most of them, connected with the ancestral worship of the sovereigns of the Shang and Kâu dynasties, and of the marquises of Lû. Of the ancestral worship of the common people we have almost no information in the Shih. It was binding, however, on all, and two utterances of Confucius may be given in illustration of this. In the eighteenth chapter of the Doctrine of the Mean, telling how the duke of Kâu, the legislator of the dynasty so called, had 'completed the virtuous course of Wan and Wû, carrying up the title of king to Wan's father and grandfather, and sacrificing to the dukes before them with the royal ceremonies,' he adds, And this rule he extended to the feudal princes, the great officers, the other officers, and the common people. In the mourning and other duties rendered to a deceased father or mother, he allowed no difference between the noble and the mean. Again, his summary in the tenth chapter of the Hsiâo

King, of the duties of filial piety, is the following:—'A filial son, in serving his parents, in his ordinary intercourse with them, should show the utmost respect; in supplying them with food, the greatest delight; when they are ill, the utmost solicitude; when mourning for their death, the deepest grief; and when sacrificing to them, the profoundest solemnity. When these things are all complete, he is able to serve his parents.'

The royal worship of ancestors.

Of the ceremonies in the royal worship of ancestors, and perhaps on some other occasions, we have much information in the pieces of this Part, and in many others in the second and third Parts. They were preceded by fasting and various purifications on the part of the king and the parties who were to assist in the performance of them. The was a great concourse of the feudal princes, and much importance was attached to the presence among them of the representatives of former dynasties; but the duties of the occasion devolved mainly on the princes of the same surname as the royal House. Libations of fragrant spirits were made, especially in the Kâu period, to attract the Spirits, and their presence was invoked by a functionary who took his place inside the principal gate. The principal victim, a red bull in the temple of Kâu, was killed by the king himself, using for the purpose a knife to the handle of which small bells were attached. With this he laid bare the hair, to show that the animal was of the required colour, inflicted the wound of death, and cut away the fat, which was burned along with southernwood to increase the incense and fragrance. Other victims were numerous, and the fifth ode of the second decade, Part II, describes all engaged in the service as greatly exhausted with what they had to do, flaying the carcases, boiling the flesh, roasting it, broiling it, arranging it on trays and stands, and setting it forth. Ladies from the palace are present to give their assistance; music peals; the cup goes round. The description is that of a feast as much as of a sacrifice; and in fact, those great seasonal occasions were what we might call grand family reunions, where the dead and the living met, eating and drinking together, where the living worshipped the dead, and the dead blessed the living.

This characteristic of these ceremonies appeared most strikingly in the custom which required that the departed ancestors should be represented by living relatives of the same surname, chosen according to certain rules that are not mentioned in the Shih.. These took for the time the place of the dead, received the honours which were due to them, and were supposed to be possessed by their spirits. They ate and drank as those whom they personated would have done; accepted for them the homage rendered by their descendants; communicated their will to the principal in the service, and pronounced on him and on his line their benediction, being assisted in this point by a mediating priest, as we may call him for want of a more exact term. On the next day, after a summary repetition of the ceremonies of the sacrifice, those personators of the dead were specially feasted, and, as it is expressed in the second decade of Part III, ode 4, 'their happiness and dignity were made complete.' We have an allusion to this strange custom in Mencius (VI, i, ch. 5), showing how a junior member of a family, when chosen to represent one of his ancestors, was for the time exalted above his elders, and received the demonstrations of reverence due to the ancestor.

When the sacrifice to ancestors was finished, the king feasted his uncles and younger brothers or cousins, that is, all the princes and nobles of the same surname with himself, in another apartment. The musicians who had discoursed with instrument and voice during the worship and entertainment of the ancestors, followed the convivial party 'to give their soothing aid at the second blessing.' The viands that had been provided, we have seen, in great abundance, were brought in from the temple, and set forth anew. The guests ate to the full and drank to the full, and at the conclusion they all did obeisance, while one of them declared the satisfaction of the Spirits, and assured the king of their favour to him and his posterity, so long as they did not neglect those observances. During the feast the king showed particular respect to those among his relatives who were aged filled their cups again and again, and desired 'that their old age might be blessed, and their bright happiness ever increased.'

The above sketch of the seasonal sacrifices to ancestors shows that they were intimately related to the duty of filial piety, and were designed mainly to maintain the unity of the family connexion.

35

There was implied in them a belief in the continued existence of the spirits of the departed; and by means of them the ancestors of the kings were raised to the position of the Tutelary spirits of the dynasty; and the ancestors of each family became its Tutelary spirits. Several of the pieces in Part IV are appropriate, it will be observed, to sacrifices offered to some one monarch. They would be used on particular occasions connected with his achievements in the past, or when it was supposed that his help would be valuable in contemplated enterprises. With regard to all the ceremonies of the ancestral temple, Confucius gives the following account of the purposes which they were intended to serve, hardly adverting to their religious significance, in the nineteenth chapter of the Doctrine of the Mean:—'By means of them they distinguished the royal kindred according to their order of descent. By arranging those present according to their rank, they distinguished the more noble and the less. By the apportioning of duties at them, they made a distinction of talents and worth. In the ceremony of general pledging, the inferiors presented the cup to their superiors, and thus something was given to the lowest to do. At the (concluding) feast places were given according to the hair, and thus was marked the distinction of years.'

The worship paid to God.

The Shih does not speak of the worship which was paid to God, unless it be incidentally. There were two grand occasions on which it was rendered by the sovereign,—the summer and winter solstices. These two sacrifices were offered on different altars, that in winter being often described as offered to Heaven, and that in summer to Earth; but we have the testimony of Confucius, in the nineteenth chapter of the Doctrine of the Mean, that the object of them both was to serve Shang-Tî. Of the ceremonies on these two occasions, however, I do not speak here, as there is nothing said about them in the Shih. But there were other sacrifices to God, at stated periods in the course of the year, of at least two of which we have some intimation in the pieces of this fourth Part. The last in the first decade of the Sacrificial Odes of Kâu is addressed to Hâu Kî as having proved himself the correlate of Heaven, in teaching men to cultivate the grain which God had appointed for the nourishment of all. This was appropriate to a sacrifice in spring, offered to God to seek His blessing on the agricultural labours of the year, Hâu Kî, as the ancestor of the House of Kâu, being associated with Him in it. The seventh piece of the same decade again was appropriate to a sacrifice to God in autumn, in the Hall of Light, at a great audience to the feudal princes, when king Wan was associated with Him as being the founder of the dynasty of Kâu.

With these preliminary observations to assist the reader in understanding the pieces in this Part, I proceed to give—

1. THE SACRIFICIAL ODES OF SHANG.

THESE Odes of Shang constitute the last Book in the ordinary editions of the Shih. I put them here in the first place, because they are the oldest pieces in the collection. There are only five of them.

The sovereigns of the dynasty of Shang who occupied the throne from B.C. 1766 to 1123. They traced their lineage to Hsieh, appears in the Shû as Minister of Instruction to Shun. By Yâo or by Shun, Hsieh was invested with the principality of Shang, corresponding to the small department which is so named in Shen-hsi. Fourteenth in descent from him came Thien-Yî, better known as Khang Thang, or Thang the Successful, who dethroned the last descendant of the line of Hsiâ, and became the founder of a new dynasty. We meet with him first at a considerable distance from the ancestral fief (which, however, gave name to the dynasty), having as his capital the southern Po, which seems correctly referred to the present district of Shang-khiû, in the department of Kwei-teh, Ho-nan. Among the twenty-seven sovereigns who followed Thang, there were three especially distinguished:—Thâi Kiâ, his grandson and successor (B.C. 1753 to 1721), who received the title of Thai Zung; Thai Mâu (B.C. 1637 to 1563), canonized as Kung Zung; and Wû-ting (B.C. 1324 to 1266), known as Kâo Zung. The shrines of these three sovereigns and that of Thang retained their places in the ancestral temple ever after they were first set up and if all the sacrificial odes of the dynasty had been preserved, most of them would have been in praise of one or other of the four. But it so happened that at least all the odes of which Thai Zung was the subject were lost, and of the others we have only the small portion that has been mentioned above.

Of how it is that we have even these, we have the following account in the Narratives of the States, compiled, probably, by a contemporary of Confucius. The count of Wei was made duke of Sung by king Wû of Kâu, as related in the Shû, V, viii, there to continue the sacrifices of the House of Shang; but the government of Sung fell subsequently into disorder, and the memorials of the dynasty were lost. In the time of duke Tâi (B.C. 799 to 766), one of his ministers, Kang-khâo, an ancestor of Confucius, received from the Grand Music-Master at the court of Kâu twelve of the sacrificial odes of Shang with which he returned to Sung, where they were used in sacrificing to the old Shang kings. It is supposed that seven of these were lost subsequently, before the collection of the Shih was formed.

ODE 1. THE NÂ [1].

APPROPRIATE TO A SACRIFICE TO THANG, THE FOUNDER OF THE SHANG DYNASTY, DWELLING ESPECIALLY ON THE MUSIC AND THE REVERENCE WITH WHICH THE SACRIFICE WAS PERFORMED.

We cannot tell by which of the kings of Shang the sacrifice here referred to was first performed. He is simply spoken of as 'a descendant of Thang.' The ode seems to have been composed by some one, probably a member of the royal House, who had taken part in the service.

How admirable! how complete! Here are set our hand-drums and drums. The drums resound harmonious and loud, To delight our meritorious ancestor [2].

The descendant of Thang invites him with this music, That he may soothe us with the realization of our thoughts [3]. Deep is the sound of our hand-

1. The piece is called the Nâ, because a character so named is an important part of the first line. So generally the pieces in the Shih receive their names from a character or phrase occurring in them. This point will not be again touched on.
2. The 'meritorious ancestor' is Thang. The sacrifices of the Shang dynasty commenced with music; those of the Kâu with libations of fragrant spirits;—in both cases with the same object, to attract the spirit, or spirits, sacrificed to, and secure their presence at the service. Khan Hâo (Ming dynasty) says, 'The departed

spirits hover between heaven and earth, and sound goes forth, filling the region of the air. Hence in sacrificing, the people of Yin began with a performance of music.'

3. The Lî Kî, XXIV, i, parr. 2, 3, tells us, that the sacrificer, as preliminary to the service, had to fast for some days, and to think of the person of his ancestor,—where he had stood and sat, how he had smiled and spoken, what had been his cherished aims, pleasures, and delights; and on the third day he would have a complete image of him in his mind's eye. Then on the day of sacrifice, when he entered the temple, he would seem to see him in his shrine, and to hear him, as he went about in the discharge of the service. This line seems to indicate the realization of all this.

drums and drums; Shrilly sound the flutes; All harmonious and blending together, According to the notes of the sonorous gem. Oh! majestic is the descendant of Thang; Very admirable is his music.

The large bells and drums fill the ear; The various dances are grandly performed[1]. We have the admirable visitors[2], who are pleased and delighted.

From of old, before our time, The former men set us the example;—How to be mild and humble from morning to night, And to be reverent in discharging the service.

May he regard our sacrifices of winter and autumn[3], (Thus) offered by the descendant of Thang!

ODE 2. THE LIEH ZÛ.

PROBABLY LIKE THE LAST ODE, APPROPRIATE TO A SACRIFICE TO THANG, DWELLING ON THE SPIRITS, THE SOUP, AND THE GRAVITY OF THE SERVICE, AND ON THE ASSISTING PRINCES.

Neither can we tell by which of the kings of Shang this ode was first used. Kû Hsî says that the object of the sacrifice was Thang. The Preface assigns it to Thâi Mâu, the Kung Zung, or second of the three 'honoured Ones.' But there is not a

1. Dancing thus entered into the service as an accompaniment of the music. Two terms are employed; one denoting the movements appropriate to a dance Of war, the other those appropriate to a dance of peace.
2. The visitors would be the representatives of the lines of Hsiâ, Shun, and Yâo.
3. Two of the seasonal sacrifices are thus specified, by synecdoche, for all the four.

word in praise of Fung Zung, and the 'meritorious ancestor' of the first line is not to be got over. Still more clearly than in the case of the former ode does this appear to have been made by some one who had taken part in the service, for in line 4 he addresses the sacrificing king as 'you.'

Ah! ah! our meritorious ancestor! Permanent are the blessings coming from him, Repeatedly conferred without end;—They have come to you in this place.

The clear spirits are in our vessels, And there is granted to us the realization of our thoughts. There are also the well-tempered soups, Prepared beforehand, with the ingredients rightly proportioned. By these offerings we invite his presence, without a word, Without (unseemly) contention (among the worshippers). He will bless us with the eyebrows of longevity, With the grey hair and wrinkled face in unlimited degree.

With the naves of their wheels bound with leather, and their ornamented yokes, With the eight bells at their horses' bits all tinkling, (The princes) come to assist at the offerings[1]. We have received the appointment in all its greatness, And from Heaven is our prosperity sent down, Fruitful years of great abundance. (Our ancestor) will come and enjoy (our offerings), And confer on us happiness without limit.

May he regard our sacrifices of winter and autumn, (Thus) offered by the descendant of Thang!

1. These lines are descriptive of the feudal princes, who were present and assisted at the sacrificial service. The chariot of each was drawn by four horses yoked abreast, two insides and two outsides, on each side of the bits of which small bells were attached.

ODE 3. THE HSÜAN NIÂO

APPROPRIATE TO A SACRIFICE IN THE ANCESTRAL TEMPLE OF SHANG;—INTENDED SPECIALLY TO DO HONOUR TO THE KING WÛ-TING.

If this ode were not intended to do honour to Wû-ting, the Kâo Zung of Shang, we cannot account for the repeated mention of him in it. Kû Hsî, however, in his note on it, says nothing about Wû-ting, but simply that the piece belonged to the sacrifices in the ancestral temple, tracing back the line of the kings of Shang to its origin, and to its attaining the sovereignty of the kingdom. Not at all unlikely is the view of Kang Hsüan, that the sacrifice was in the third year after the death of Wû-ting and offered to him in the temple of Hsieh, the ancestor of the Shang dynasty.

Heaven commissioned the swallow, To descend and give birth to (the father of our) Shang[1]. (His descendants) dwelt in the land of Yin, and became great. (Then) long ago God appointed the martial Thang, To regulate the boundaries throughout the four quarters (of the kingdom).

(In those) quarters he appointed the princes, And grandly possessed the nine regions[2]. The

1. The father of Shang is Hsieh, who has already been mentioned. The mother of Hsieh was a daughter of the House of the ancient state of Sung, and a concubine of the ancient ruler Khû (B.C. 2435). According to Mâo, she accompanied Khû, at the time of the vernal equinox, when the swallow made its appearance, to sacrifice and pray to the first match-maker, and the result was the birth of Hsieh. Sze-mâ Khien and Kang make Hsieh's birth more marvellous:—The lady was bathing in some open place, when a swallow made its appearance, and dropt an egg, which she took and swallowed; and from this came Hsieh. The editors of the imperial edition of the Shih, of the present dynasty, say we need not believe the legends;—the important point is to believe that the birth of Hsieh was specially ordered by Heaven.
2 'The nine regions' are the nine provinces into which Yü divided the kingdom.

first sovereign of Shang[1] Received the appointment without any element of instability in it, And it is (now) held by the descendant of Wû-ting [2].

The descendant of Wû-ting Is a martial sovereign, equal to every emergency. Ten princes, (who came) with their dragon-emblazoned banners, Bear the large dishes of millet.

The royal domain of a thousand lî Is where the people rest; But the boundaries that reach to the four seas commence there.

From the four seas [3] they come (to our sacrifices); They come in multitudes. King has the Ho for its outer border [4]. That Yin[5] should have received the appointment (of Heaven) was entirely right; (Its sovereign) sustains all its dignities.

ODE 4. THE KHANG FÂ.

CELEBRATING HSIEH, THE ANCESTOR OF THE HOUSE OF SHANG; HSIANG-THÛ, HIS GRANDSON; THANG, THE FOUNDER OF THE DYNASTY; AND Î-YIN, THANG'S CHIEF MINISTER AND ADVISER.

It does not appear on occasion of what sacrifice this piece was made. The most probable view is that of Mâo, that it was the

1. That is, Thang.
2. If this ode were used, as Mang supposes, in the third year after Wû-ting's death, this ' descendant' would be his son Zû-kang, B.C. 1265 to 1259.
3. This expression, which occurs also in the Shû, indicates that the early Chinese believed that their country extended to the sea, east, west, north, and south.
4. Kû Hsî Says he did not understand this line; but there is ground in the Zo Kwan for our believing that King was the name of a hill in the region where the capital of Shang was.
5. We saw in the Shû that the name Shang gave place to Yin after the time of Pan-kang, B.C. 1401 to 1374. Wû-ting's reign was subsequent to that of Pan-kang.

'great Tî sacrifice,' when the principal object of honour would be the ancient Khû, the father of Hsieh, with Hsieh as his correlate, and all the kings of the dynasty, with the earlier lords of Shang, and their famous ministers and advisers, would have their places at the service. I think this is the oldest of the odes of Shang.

Profoundly wise were (the lords of) Shang, And long had there appeared the omens (of their dignity).

When the waters of the deluge spread vast abroad, Yû arranged and divided the regions of the land, And assigned to the exterior great states their boundaries, With their borders extending all over (the kingdom). (Even) then the chief of Sung was beginning to be great, And God raised up the son (of his daughter), and founded (the line of) Shang[1].

The dark king exercised an effective sway[2]. Charged with a small state, he commanded success: Charged with a large state, he commanded success[3]. He followed his rules of conduct without error; Wherever he inspected (the people), they responded (to his instructions[4]. (Then came) Hsiang-thû all ardent [5], And all within the four seas, beyond (the middle regions), acknowledged his restraints.

1. This line refers to the birth of Hsieh, as described in the previous ode, and his being made lord of Shang.
2. It would be hard to say why Hsieh is here called 'the dark king.' There may be an allusion to the legend about the connexion of the swallow,—'the dark bird,'—with his birth, He never was 'a king;' but his descendants here represented him as such.
3. All that is meant here is, that the territory of Shang was enlarged under Hsieh.
4. There is a reference here to Hsieh's appointment by Shun to be Minister of Instruction.
5. Hsiang-thû appears in the genealogical lists as grandson of Hsieh. We know nothing of him but what is related here.

The favour of God did not leave (Shang), And in Thang was found the fit object for its display. Thang was not born too late, And his wisdom and reverence daily advanced:—Brilliant was the influence of his character (on Heaven) for long. God he revered, And God appointed him to be the model for the nine regions.

He received the rank-tokens of the states, small and large, Which depended on him like the pendants of a banner:—So did he receive the blessing of Heaven. He was neither violent nor remiss, Neither hard nor soft. Gently he spread his instructions abroad, And all dignities and riches were concentrated in him.

He received the tribute of the states, small and large, And he supported them as a strong steed (does its burden):—So did he receive the favour of Heaven. He displayed everywhere his valour, Unshaken, unmoved, Unterrified, unscared:—All dignities were united in him.

The martial king displayed his banner, And with reverence grasped his axe. It was like (the case of) a blazing fire which no one can repress. The root, with its three shoots, Could make no progress, no growth[1]. The nine regions were effectually secured by Thang. Having smitten (the princes of) Wei and Kû, He dealt with (him of) Kün-wû and with Kieh of Hsiâ.

Formerly, in the middle of the period (before

1. By 'the root' we are to understand Thang's chief opponent, Kieh, the last king of Hsiâ. Kieh's three great helpers were 'the three shoots,'—the princes of Wei, Kû, and Kün-wû; but the exact sites of their principalities cannot be made out.

Thang), There was a time of shaking and peril[1]. But truly did Heaven (then) deal with him as a son, And sent him down a high minister, Namely, Â-hang[2], Who gave his assistance to the king of Shang.

43

ODE 5. THE YIN WÛ.

CELEBRATING THE WAR OF WÛ-TING AGAINST KING-KHÛ, ITS SUCCESS, AND THE GENERAL HAPPINESS AND VIRTUE OF HIS REIGN;—MADE, PROBABLY, WHEN A SPECIAL AND PERMANENT TEMPLE WAS BUILT FOR HIM AS THE 'HIGH AND HONOURED' KING OF SHANG.

The concluding lines indicate that the temple was made on the occasion which I thus assign to it. After Wû-ting's death, his spirit-tablet would be shrined in the ancestral temple, and he would have his share in the seasonal sacrifices; but several reigns would elapse before there was any necessity to make any other arrangement, so that his tablet should not be removed, and his share in the sacrifices not be discontinued. Hence the composition of the piece has been referred to the time of Tî-yî, the last but one of the kings of Shang.

Rapid was the warlike energy of (our king of) Yin, And vigorously did he attack King-Khû [3].

1. We do not know anything of this time of decadence in the fortunes of Shang between Hsieh and Thang.
2. Â-hang is Î Yin, who plays so remarkable a part in the Shû, IV, Books iv, v, and vi.
3. King, or Khû, or King-Khû, as the two names are combined here, was a large and powerful half-savage state, having its capital in the present Wû-pei. So far as evidence goes, we should say, but for this ode, that the name of Khû was not in use till long after the Shang dynasty. The name King appears several times in 'the Spring and Autumn' in the annals of duke Kwang (B.C. 693 to 662), and then it gives place to the name Khû in the first year of duke Hsî (B.C. 659), and subsequently disappears itself altogether. In consequence of this some critics make this piece out to have been composed under the Kâu dynasty. The point cannot be fully cleared up; but on the whole I accept the words of the ode as sufficient proof against the silence of other documents.

Boldly he entered its dangerous passes, And brought the multitudes of King together, Till the country was reduced under complete restraint: Such was the fitting achievement of the descendant of Thang!

'Ye people,' (he said), 'of King-Khû, Dwell in the southern part of my kingdom. Formerly, in the time of Thang the Successful, Even from the Kiang of Tî[1], They dared not but come with their offerings; (Their chiefs) dared not but come to seek acknowledgment[2]:—Such is the regular rule of Shang.'

Heaven had given their appointments (to the princes), But where their capitals, had been assigned within the sphere of the labours of Yü, For the business of every year they appeared before our king[3], (Saying), 'Do not punish nor reprove us; We have not been remiss in our husbandry.'

When Heaven by its will is inspecting (the kingdom), The lower people are to be feared. (Our king) showed no partiality (in rewarding), no excess (in punishing); He dared not to allow himself in indolence:—So was his appointment (established)

1. The Tî Kiang, or Kiang of Tî, still existed in the time of the Han dynasty, occupying portions of the present Kan-sû.
2. The chiefs of the wild tribes, lying beyond the nine provinces of the kingdom, were required to present themselves once in their lifetime at the royal court. The rule, in normal periods, was for each chief to appear immediately after he had succeeded to the headship of his tribe.
3. The feudal lords had to appear at court every year. They did so, we may suppose, at the court of Wû-ting, the more so because of his subjugation of King-Khû.

over the states, And he made his happiness grandly secure.

The capital of Shang was full of order, The model for all parts of the kingdom. Glorious was (the king's) fame; Brilliant his energy. Long lived he and enjoyed tranquillity, And so he preserves us, his descendants.

We ascended the hill of King[1], Where the pines and cypresses grew symmetrical. We cut them down and conveyed them here; We reverently hewed them square. Long are the projecting beams of pine; Large are the many pillars. The temple was completed,—the tranquil abode (of the martial king of Yin).

II. THE SACRIFICIAL ODES OF KÂU.

IN this division we have thirty one sacrificial odes of Kâu, arranged in three decades, the third of which, however, contains eleven pieces. They belong mostly to the time of king Wan, the founder of the Kâu dynasty, and to the reigns of his son and grandson, kings Wû and Khang. The decades are named from the name of the first piece in each.

The First Decade, or that of Khing Miâo.

ODE 1. THE KHING MIÂO.

CELEBRATING THE REVERENTIAL MANNER IN WHICH A SACRIFICE TO KING WAN; WAS PERFORMED, AND FURTHER PRAISING HIM.

Chinese critics agree in assigning this piece to the sacrifice mentioned in the Shû, in the end of the thirteenth Book of Part V, when, the building of Lo being finished, king Khang came to

1. See on the last line but two of ode 3.

the new city, and offered a red bull to Wǎn, and the same to Wû. It seems to me to have been sung in honour of Wǎn, after the service was completed. This determination of the occasion of the piece being accepted, we should refer it to B.C. 1108.

Oh! solemn is the ancestral temple in its pure stillness. Reverent and harmonious were the distinguished assistants[1]; Great was the number of the officers [2]:—(All) assiduous followers of the virtue of (king Wǎn). In response to him in heaven, Grandly they hurried about in the temple. Distinguished is he and honoured, And will never be wearied of among men.

ODE 2. THE WEI THIEN KIH MING.

CELEBRATING THE VIRTUE OF KING WAN AS COMPARABLE TO THAT OF HEAVEN, AND LOOKING TO HIM FOR BLESSING IN THE FUTURE.

According to the Preface, there is an announcement here of the realization of complete peace throughout the kingdom, and some of the old critics refer the ode to a sacrifice to king Wǎn by the duke of Kâu, when he had completed the statutes for the new dynasty. But there is nothing to authorize a more definite argument of the contents than I have given.

The ordinances of Heaven,—How deep are they and unintermitting! And oh! how illustrious Was the singleness of the virtue of king Wan [3]!

How does he (now) show his kindness? We will receive it, Striving to be in accord with him, our

1. These would be the princes who were assembled on the occasion, and assisted the king in the service.
2. That is, the officers who took part in the libations, prayers, and other parts of the sacrifice.
3. See what Dze-sze says on these four lines in the Doctrine of the Mean, XXVI, par. 10.

king Wan; And may his remotest descendant be abundantly the same!

ODE 3. THE WEI KHING.

APPROPRIATE AT SOME SACRIFICE TO KING WAN, AND CELEBRATING HIS STATUTES.

Nothing more can, with any likelihood of truth, be said of this short piece, which moreover has the appearance of being a fragment.

Clear and to be preserved bright, Are the statutes of king Wan. From the first sacrifice (to him), Till now when they have issued in our complete state, They have been the happy omen of (the fortunes of) Kâu.

ODE 4. THE LIEH WAN.

A SONG IN PRAISE OF THE PRINCES WHO HAVE ASSISTED AT A SACRIFICE, AND ADMONISHING THEM.

The Preface says that this piece was made on the occasion of king Khang's accession to the government, when he thus addressed the princes who had assisted him in the ancestral temple. Kû Hsî considers that it was a piece for general use in the ancestral temple, to be sung when the king presented a cup to his assisting guests, after they had thrice presented the cup to the representatives of the dead. There is really nothing in it to enable us to decide in favour of either view.

Ye, brilliant and accomplished princes, Have conferred on me this happiness. Your favours to me are without limit, And my descendants will preserve (the fruits of) them.

Be not mercenary nor extravagant in your states, And the king will honour you. Thinking of this service, He will enlarge the dignity of your successors.

What is most powerful is the being the man:—Its influence will be felt throughout your states. What is most distinguished is the being virtuous:—It will secure the imitation of all the princes. Ah! the former kings cannot be forgotten!

ODE 5. THE THIEN ZO.

APPROPRIATE TO A SACRIFICE TO KING THÂI.

We cannot tell what the sacrifice was; and the Preface, indeed, says that the piece was used in the seasonal sacrifices to all the former king., s and dukes of the House of Kâu. King Thâi was the grandfather of king Wan, and, before he received that title, was known as 'the ancient duke Than-fû.' In B.C. 1327, he moved with his followers from Pin, an earlier seat of his House, and settled in the plain of Khî, about fifty lî to the north-east of the present district city of Khî-shan, in Shen-hsî.

Heaven made the lofty hill[1], And king Thâi brought (the country about) it under cultivation. He made the commencement with it, And king Wan tranquilly (carried on the work), (Till) that rugged (mount) Khî Had level roads leading to it. May their descendants ever preserve it!

ODE 6. THE HÂO THIEN YÛ KHANG MING.

APPROPRIATE TO A SACRIFICE TO KING KHANG.

Khang was the honorary title of Sung, the son and successor of king Wû, B.C. 1115 to 1079.

Heaven made its determinate appointment, which our two sovereigns received[2]. King Khang did not dare to rest idly in it, But night and day enlarged

1. Meaning mount Khî.
2. Wan and Wû.

its foundations by his deep and silent virtue. How did he continue and glorify (his heritage), Exerting all his heart, And so securing its tranquillity!

ODE 7. THE WÛ KIANG.

APPROPRIATE TO A SACRIFICE TO KING WAN, ASSOCIATED WITH HEAVEN, IN THE HALL OF AUDIENCE.

There is, happily, an agreement among the critics as to the occasion to which this piece is referred. It took place in the last month of autumn, in the Hall of Audience, called also 'the Brilliant Hall,' and 'the Hall of Light.' We must suppose that the princes are all assembled at court, and that the king receives them in this hall. A sacrifice is then presented to God, with him is associated king Wan, and the two being the fountain from which, and the channel through which, the sovereignty had come to Kâu.

I have brought my offerings, A ram and a bull. May Heaven accept them[1]!

I imitate and follow and observe the statutes of king Wan, Seeking daily to secure the tranquillity of the kingdom. King Wan, the Blesser, has descended on the right, and accepted (the offerings).

Do I not, night and day, Revere the majesty of Heaven, Thus to preserve (its favour).

ODE 8. THE SHIH MÂI.

APPROPRIATE TO KING WÛ'S SACRIFICING TO HEAVEN, AND TO THE SPIRITS OF THE HILLS AND RIVERS, ON A PROGRESS THROUGH THE KINGDOM, AFTER THE OVERTHROW OF THE SHANG DYNASTY.

Here again there is an agreement among the critics. We find from the Zo Kwan and 'the Narratives of the States.' that the

1. This is a prayer. The worshipper, it is in view of the majesty of Heaven, shrank from assuming that God would certainly accept his sacrifice. He assumes, below, that king Wan does so.

piece was, when those compilations were made, considered to be the work of the duke of Kâu; and, no doubt, it was made by him soon after the accession of Wû to the kingdom, and when he was making a royal progress in assertion of his being appointed by Heaven to succeed to the rulers of Shang. The 'I' in the fourteenth line is, most probably, to be taken of the duke of Kâu, who may have recited the piece on occasion of the sacrifices, in the hearing of the assembled princes and lords.

Now is he making a progress through his states; May Heaven deal with him as its son!

Truly are the honour and succession come from it to the House of Kâu. To his movements All respond with tremulous awe. He has attempted and given rest to all spiritual beings [1], Even to (the spirits of) the Ho and the highest hills. Truly is the king our sovereign lord.

Brilliant and illustrious is the House of Kâu. He has regulated the positions of the princes; He has called in shields and spears; He has returned to their cases bows and arrows[2]. He will cultivate admirable virtue, And display it throughout these great regions. Truly will the king preserve the appointment.

1. 'All spiritual beings' is, literally, 'the hundred spirits,' meaning the spirits presiding, under Heaven, over all nature, and especially the spirits of the rivers and hills throughout the kingdom. Those of the Ho and the lofty mountains are mentioned, because if their spirits were satisfied with Wû, those of all other mountains and hills, no doubt, were so.
2. Compare with these lines the last chapter of 'the Completion of the War' in the Shû.

ODE 9. THE KIH KING.

AN ODE APPROPRIATE IN SACRIFICING TO THE KINGS WÛ, KHANG, AND KHANG.

The Chinese critics differ in the interpretation of this ode, the Preface and older scholars restricting it to a sacrifice to king Wû, while Kû Hsî and others find reference in it, as to me also seems most natural, to Khang and Khang, who succeeded him.

The arm of king Wû was full of strength; Irresistible was his ardour. Greatly illustrious were Khang and Khang [1], Kinged by God.

When we consider how Khang and Khang Grandly held all within the four quarters (of the kingdom), How penetrating was their intelligence!

The bells and drums sound in harmony; The sounding-stones and flutes blend their notes; Abundant blessing is sent down.

Blessing is sent down in large measure. Careful and exact is all our deportment; We have drunk, and we have eaten, to the fall; Our happiness and dignity will be prolonged.

ODE 10. THE SZE WAN.

APPROPRIATE TO ONE OF THE BORDER SACRIFICES, WHEN HÂU-KÎ WAS WORSHIPPED AS THE CORRELATE OF GOD, AND CELEBRATING HIM.

Hâu-kî was the same as Khî, who appears in Part II of the Shû as Minister of Agriculture to Yâo and Shun, and co-operating with

1. If the whole piece be understood only of a sacrifice to Wû, this line will have to be translated—'How illustrious was he, who completed (his great work), and secured its tranquillity.' We must deal similarly with the next line. This construction is very forced; nor is the text clear on the view of Kû-Hsî.

Yü in his labours on the flooded land. The name Hâu belongs to him as lord of Thâi; that of Ki, as Minister of Agriculture. However the combination arose, Hâu-kî became historically the name of Khî of the time of Yâo and Shun, the ancestor to whom the kings of Kâu traced their lineage. He was to the people the Father of Husbandry, who first taught men to plough and sow and reap. Hence, when the kings offered sacrifice and prayer to God at the commencement of spring for his blessing on the labours of the year, they associated Hâu-kî with him at the service.

O accomplished Hâu-kî, Thou didst prove thyself the correlate of Heaven. Thou didst give grain-food to our multitudes:—The immense gift of thy goodness. Thou didst confer on us the wheat and the barley, Which God appointed for the nourishment of all. And without distinction of territory or boundary, The rules of social duty were diffused throughout these great regions.

The Second Decade, or that of Khan Kung.

ODE 1. THE KHAN KUNG.

INSTRUCTIONS GIVEN TO THE OFFICERS OF HUSBANDRY.

The place of this piece among the sacrificial odes makes us assign it to the conclusion of some sacrifice; but what the sacrifice was we cannot tell. The Preface says that it was addressed, at the conclusion of the spring sacrifice to ancestors to the princes who had been present and taken part in the service. Kû Hsî says nothing but what I have stated in the above argument of the piece.

Ah! ah! ministers and officers, Reverently attend to your public duties. The king has given you perfect rules;—Consult about them and consider them.

Ah! ah! ye assistants.. It is now the end of spring [1]; And what have ye to seek for? (Only) how to manage the new fields and those of the third year, How beautiful are the wheat and the barley! The bright and glorious God Will in them give us a good year. Order all our men To be provided with their spuds and hoes:—Anon we shall see the sickles at work.

ODE 2. THE Î HSÎ.

FURTHER INSTRUCTIONS TO THE OFFICERS OF HUSBANDRY.

Again there is a difficulty in determining to what sacrifice this piece should be referred. The Preface says it was sung on the occasions of sacrifice by the king to God, in spring and summer, for a good year. But the note on the first two lines will show that this view cannot be accepted without modification.

Oh! yes, king Khang [2] Brightly brought himself near [2]. Lead your husbandmen To sow their various kinds of grain, Going vigorously to work

1. It is this line which makes it difficult to determine after what sacrifice we are to suppose these instructions to have been delivered. The year, during the Hsiâ dynasty, began with the first month of spring, as it now does in China, in consequence of Confucius having said that that was the proper time. Under the Shang dynasty, it commenced a month earlier; and during the Kâu period, it ought always to have begun with the new moon preceding the winter solstice,—between our November 22 and December 22. But in the writings of the Kâu period we find statements of time continually referred to the calendar of Hsiâ,—as here.
2. These first two lines are all but unmanageable. The old critics held that there was no mention of king Khang in them; but the text is definite on this point. We must suppose that a special service had been performed at his shrine, asking him to intimate the day when the sacrifice after which the instructions were given should be performed; and that a directing oracle had been received.

on your private fields[1], All over the thirty lî[2]. Attend to your ploughing, With your ten thousand men all in pairs.

ODE 3. THE KÂU LÛ.

CELEBRATING THE REPRESENTATIVES OF FORMER DYNASTIES, WHO HAD COME TO COURT TO ASSIST AT A SACRIFICE IN THE ANCESTRAL TEMPLE.

This piece may have been used when the king was dismissing his distinguished guests in the ancestral temple. See the introductory note to this Part, pp. 300, 301.

A flock of egrets is flying, About the marsh there in the west[3]. My visitors came, With an (elegant) carriage like those birds.

There, (in their states), not disliked, Here, (in Kâu), never tired of;-They are sure, day and night, To perpetuate their fame.

1. The mention of 'the private fields' implies that there were also 'the public fields,' cultivated by the husbandmen in common, in behalf of the government. As the people are elsewhere introduced, wishing that the rain might first fall on 'the public fields,' to show their loyalty, so the king here mentions only 'the private fields,' to show his sympathy and consideration for the people.
2. For the cultivation of the ground, the allotments of single families were separated by a small ditch; ten allotments, by a larger; a hundred, by what we may call a brook; a thousand, by a small stream; and ten thousand, by a river. The space occupied by 10,000 families formed a square of a little more than thirty-two lî. We may suppose that this space was intended by the round number of thirty lî in the text. So at least Kang Khang-kang explained it.
3. These two lines make the piece allusive. See the Introduction, p. 279.

ODE 4. THE FANG NIEN.

AN ODE OF THANKSGIVING FOR A PLENTIFUL YEAR.

The Preface says the piece was used at sacrifices in autumn and winter. Kû Hsî calls it an ode of thanksgiving for a good year,—without any specification of time. He supposes, however, that the thanks were given to the ancient Shan-nang, 'the father of Agriculture,' Hâu-kî, 'the first Husbandman,' and the spirits presiding over the four quarters of the heavens. To this the imperial editors rightly demur, saying that the blessings which the piece speaks of could come only from God.

Abundant is the year with much millet and much rice And we have our high granaries, With myriads, and hundreds of thousands, and millions (of measures in them); For spirits and sweet spirits, To present to our forefathers, male and female, And to supply all our ceremonies. The blessings sent down on us are of every kind.

ODE 5. THE YÛ KÛ.

THE BLIND MUSICIANS OF THE COURT OF KÂU; THE INSTRUMENT OF MUSIC; AND THEIR HARMONY.

The critics agree in holding that this piece was made on occasion of the duke of Kâu's completing his instruments of music for the ancestral, temple, and announcing the fact at a grand performance in the temple of king Wan. It cam hardly be regarded as a sacrificial ode.

There are the blind musicians; there are the blind musicians; In the court of (the temple of) Kâu.[1]

1. The blind musicians at the court of Kâu were numerous. The blindness of the eyes was supposed to make the ears more acute in hearing, and to be favourable to the powers of the voice. In the Official Book of Kâu, III, i, par. 22, the enumeration of these blind musicians gives 2 directors of the first rank, and 4 of the second; 40 performers of the first grade, 100 of the second, and 160 of the third; with 300 assistants who were possessed of vision. But it is difficult not to be somewhat incredulous as to this great collection of blind musicians about the court of Kâu.

There are (the music-frames with their) face-boards and posts, The high toothed-edge (of the former), and the feathers stuck (in the latter); With the drums, large and small, suspended from them; And the hand-drums and sounding-stones, the instrument to give the signal for commencing, and the stopper. These being all complete, the music is struck up. The pan-pipe and the double flute begin at the same time [1].

Harmoniously blend their sounds; In solemn unison they give forth their notes. Our ancestors will give ear. Our visitors will be there;   Long to witness the complete performance.

ODE 6. THE KHIEN.

SUNG IN THE LAST MONTH OF WINTER, AND IN SPRING, WHEN THE KING PRESENTED A FISH IN THE ANCESTRAL TEMPLE.

Such is the argument of this piece given in the Preface, and in which the critics generally concur. In the Lî Kî, IV, vi, 49, it is recorded that the king, in the third Month of winter, gave orders to his chief fisher to commence his duties, and went himself to see his operations. He partook of the fish first captured, but previously presented some as an offering in the back apartment of the ancestral temple. In the third month of spring, again, when the sturgeons began to make their appearance (Lî Kî, IV, i, 25), the king presented one in the same place. On

1. All the instruments here enumerated were performed on in the open court below the hall. Nothing is said of the stringed instruments which were used in the hall itself; nor is the enumeration of the instruments in the courtyard complete.

these passages, the prefatory notice was, no doubt, constructed. Choice specimens of the earliest-caught fish were presented by the sovereign to his ancestors, as an act of duty, and an acknowledgment that it was to their favour that he and the people were indebted for the supplies of food, which they received from the waters.

Oh! in the Khî and the Khü, There are many fish in the warrens;—Sturgeons, large and snouted, Thryssas, yellow-jaws, mud-fish, and carp;—For offerings, for sacrifice, That our bright happiness may be increased.

ODE 7. THE YUNG.

APPROPRIATE, PROBABLY, AT A SACRIFICE BY KING WÛ TO HIS FATHER WAN.

From a reference in the Analects, III, ii, to an abuse of this ode in the time of Confucius, We learn that it was sung When the sacrificial vessels and their contents were being removed.

They come full of harmony; They are here in all gravity;—
The princes assisting, While the Son of Heaven looks profound.

(He says), 'While I present (this) noble bull, And they assist me in setting forth the sacrifice, O great and august Father, Comfort me, your filial son.

With penetrating wisdom thou didst play the man. A sovereign with the gifts both of peace and war, Giving rest even to great Heaven[1], And ensuring prosperity to thy descendants.

1. To explain this line one commentator refers to the seventh stanza of the first piece in the Major Odes of the Kingdom, where it is said, 'God surveyed the four quarters of the kingdom, seeking for some one to give settlement and rest to the people;' and adds, 'Thus what Heaven has at heart is the settlement of the people, When the), have rest given to them, then Heaven is at rest.'

'Thou comfortest me with the eyebrows of longevity; Thou makest me great with manifold blessings, I offer this sacrifice to my meritorious father, And to my accomplished mother[1].'

ODE 8. THE ZÂI HSIEN.

APPROPRIATE TO AN OCCASION WHEN THE FEUDAL PRINCES HAD BEEN ASSISTING KING KHANG AT A SACRIFICE TO HIS FATHER.

They appeared before their sovereign king, To seek from him the rules (they were to observe). With their dragon-emblazoned banners, flying bright, The bells on them and their front-boards tinkling, And with the rings on the ends of the reins glittering, Admirable was their majesty and splendour.

He led them to appear before his father shrined on the left [2], Where he discharged his filial duty, and presented his offerings;— That he might have granted to him long life, And ever preserve (his dignity). Great and many are his blessings. They are the brilliant and accomplished princes, Who cheer him with his many sources of happiness,

1. At sacrifices to ancestors, the spirit tablets of wives were placed along with those of their husbands in their shrines, so that both shared in the honours of the

service. So it is now in the imperial ancestral temple in Peking. The 'accomplished mother' here would be Thâi Sze, celebrated often in the pieces of the first Book of Part I, and elsewhere.

2 Among the uses of the services of the ancestral temple, specified by Confucius and quoted on p. 302, was the distinguishing the order of descent in the royal House. According to the rules for that purpose, the characters here used enable us to determine the subject of this line as king Wû, in opposition to his father Wan.

Enabling him to perpetuate them in their brightness as pure blessing.

ODE 9. THE YÛ KHO.

CELEBRATING THE DUKE OF SUNG ON ONE OF HIS APPEARANCES AT THE CAPITAL TO ASSIST AT THE SACRIFICE IN THE ANCESTRAL TEMPLE OF KÂU;— SHOWING HOW HE WAS ESTEEMED AND CHERISHED BY THE KING.

The mention of the white horses here in the chariot of the visitor sufficiently substantiates the account in the Preface that he was the famous count of Wei, mentioned in the Shû, IV, xi, and whose subsequent investiture with the duchy of Sung, as the representative of the line of the Shang kings, is also related in the Shû, V, viii. With the dynasty of Shang white had been the esteemed and sacred colour, as red was with Kâu, and hence the duke had his carriage drawn by white horses. 'The language,' says one critic, 'is all in praise of the visitor, but it was sung in the temple, and is rightly placed therefore among the Sung.' There is, in the last line, an indication of the temple in it.

The noble visitor! The noble visitor! Drawn, like his ancestors, by white horses! The reverent and dignified, Polished members of his suite!

The noble guest will stay (but) a night or two! The noble guest will stay (but) two nights or four! Give him ropes, To bind his horses [1].

I will convoy him (with a parting feast); I will comfort him in every possible way. Adorned with such great dignity, It is very natural that he should be blessed.

1. These four lines simply express the wish of the king, to detain his visitor, from the delight that his presence gave him. Compare the similar language in the second ode of the fourth decade of Part II.

ODE 10. THE WÛ.

SUNG IN THE ANCESTRAL TEMPLE TO THE MUSIC REGULATING THE DANCE IN HONOUR OF THE ACHIEVEMENTS OF KING WÛ.

This account of the piece, given in the Preface, is variously corroborated, and has not been called in question by any critic. Perhaps this brief ode was sung as a prelude to the dance, or it may be that the seven lines are only a fragment. This, indeed, is most likely, as we have several odes in the next decade, all said to have been used at the same occasion.

Oh! great wast thou, O king Wû, Displaying the utmost strength in thy work. Truly accomplished was king Wan, Opening the path for his successors. Thou didst receive the inheritance from him. Thou didst vanquish Yin, and put a stop to its cruelties; Effecting the firm establishment of thy merit.

The Third Decade, or that of Min Yü Hsiâo Dze.

ODE 1. THE MIN YÜ.

APPROPRIATE TO THE YOUNG KING KHANG, DECLARING HIS SENTIMENTS IN THE TEMPLE OF HIS FATHER.

The speaker in this piece is, by common consent, king Khang. The only question is as to the date of its composition, whether it was made for him, in his minority, on his repairing to the temple when the mourning for his father was completed, or after the expiration of the regency of the duke of Kâu. The words 'little child,' according to their usage, are expressive of humility and not of age. They do not enable us to determine the above point.

Alas for me, who am a little child, On whom has devolved the unsettled state! Solitary am I and full of distress. Oh! my great Father, All thy life long, thou wast filial.

Thou didst think of my great grandfather, (Seeing, him, as it were) ascending and descending in the court, I, the little child, Day and night will be as reverent.

Oh! ye great kings, As your successor, I will strive not to forget you.

ODE 2. THE FANG LO.

THE YOUNG KING TELLS OF HIS DIFFICULTIES AND INCOMPETENCIES; ASKS FOR COUNSEL TO KEEP HIM TO COPY THE EXAMPLE OF HIS FATHER; STATES HOW HE MEANT TO DO SO; AND CONCLUDES WITH AN APPEAL OR PRAYER TO HIS FATHER.

This seems to be a sequel to the former ode. We can hardly say anything about it so definite as the statement in the Preface, that it relates to a council held by Khang and his ministers in the ancestral temple.

I take counsel at the beginning of my (rule), How I can follow (the example of) my shrined father. Ah! far-reaching (were his plans), And I am not yet able to carry them out. However I endeavour to reach to them, My continuation of them will still be all-deflected. I am a little child, Unequal to the many difficulties of the state. Having taken his place, (I will look for him) to go up and come down in the court, To ascend and descend in the house. Admirable art thou, O great Father, (Condescend) to preserve and enlighten me.

ODE 3. THE KING KIH.

KING KHANG SHOWS HIS SENSE OF WHAT WAS REQUIRED OF HIM TO PRESERVE THE FAVOUR OF HEAVEN, A CONSTANT JUDGE; INTIMATES HIS GOOD PURPOSES; AND ASKS THE HELP OF HIS MINISTERS TO BE ENABLED TO PERFORM THEM.

Let me be reverent! Let me be reverent! (The way of) Heaven is evident, And its appointment is not easily preserved[1]. Let me not say that it is high aloft above me. It ascends and descends about our doings; It daily inspects us wherever we are.

I am a little child, Without intelligence to be reverently (attentive to my duties); But by daily progress and monthly advance, I will learn to hold fast the gleams (of knowledge), till I arrive at bright intelligence. Assist me to bear the burden (of my position), And show me how to display a virtuous conduct.

ODE 4. THE HSIÂO PÏ.

KING KHANG ACKNOWLEDGES THAT HE HAD ERRED, AND STATES HIS PURPOSE TO HE CAREFUL IN THE FUTURE; HE WILL GUARD AGAINST THE SLIGHT BEGINNINGS OF EVIL; AND IS PENETRATED WITH A SENSE OF HIS OWN INCOMPETENCIES.

This piece has been considered by some critics as the conclusion of the council in the ancestral temple, with which the previous two also are thought to be connected. The Preface says that the king asks in it for the assistance of his ministers, but no such request is expressed. I seem myself to see in it, with Sû Khĕh and others, a reference to the suspicions which Khang at one time, we know, entertained of the fidelity of the duke of Kâu, when he was inclined to believe the rumours spread against him by his other uncles, who joined in rebellion with the son of the last king of Shang.

I condemn myself (for the past), And will be on my guard against future calamity. I will have nothing to do with a wasp, To seek for myself its painful sting. At first indeed it seemed to be

1. The meaning is this: 'The way of Heaven is very clear, to bless the good, namely, and punish the bad. But its favour is thus dependent on men themselves, and hard to preserve.'

(but) a wren[1]. But it took wing, and became a large bird. I am unequal to the many difficulties of the kingdom, And am placed in the midst of bitter experiences.

ODE 5. THE ZÂI SHÛ

THE CULTIVATION OF THE GROUND FROM THE FIRST BREAKING OF IT UP, TILL IT YIELDS ABUNDANT HARVESTS:—AVAILABLE SPECIALLY FOR SACRIFICES AND FESTIVE OCCASIONS. WHETHER INTENDED TO BE USED ON OCCASIONS OF THANKSGIVING, OR IN SPRING WHEN PRAYING FOR A GOOD YEAR, CANNOT BE DETERMINED.

The Preface says that this ode was used in spring, when the king in person turned up some furrows in the field set apart for that purpose, and prayed at the altars of the spirits of the land and the grain, for an abundant year. Ka Hsî says he does not know on what occasion it was intended to be used; but comparing it with the fourth ode of the second decade, he is inclined to rank it with that as an ode of thanksgiving. There is nothing in the piece itself to determine us in favour of either view. It brings before us a series of pleasing pictures of the husbandry of those early times. The editors of the imperial edition say that its place in the Sung makes it clear that it was an accompaniment of some royal sacrifice, We need not controvert this; but the poet evidently singled out some large estate, and describes the labour on it, from the first bringing it under cultivation to the state in which it was before his eyes, and concludes by saying that the picture which he gives of it had long been applicable to the whole country.

They clear away the grass and the bushes; And the ground is laid open by their ploughs.

In thousands of pairs they remove the roots, Some in the low wet land, some along the dykes.

1. The Chinese characters here mean, literally, 'peach-tree insect,' or, as Dr. Williams has it, 'peach-bug.' Another name for the bird is 'the clever wife,' from the artistic character of its nest, which would point it out as the small 'tailor bird.' But the name is applied to various small birds.

There are the master and his eldest son; His younger sons, and all their children; Their strong helpers, and their hired servants. How the noise of their eating the viands brought to them resounds! (The husbands) think lovingly of their wives; (The wives) keep close to their husbands. (Then) with their sharp ploughshares They set to work on the south lying acres.

They sow their various kinds of grain, Each seed containing in it a germ of life.

In unbroken lines rises the blade, And, well nourished, the stalks grow long.

Luxuriant looks the young grain, And the weeders go among it in multitudes.

Then come the reapers in crowds, And the o-rain is piled up in the fields, Myriads, and hundreds of thousands, and millions (of stacks); For spirits and for sweet spirits, To offer to our ancestors, male and female, And to provide for all ceremonies.

Fragrant is their aroma, Enhancing the glory of the state. Like pepper is their smell, To give comfort to the aged.

It is not here only that there is this (abundance); It is not now only that there is such a time:—From of old it has been thus.

ODE 6. THE LIANG SZE.

PRESUMABLY, AN ODE OF THANKSGIVING IN THE AUTUMN TO THE SPIRITS OF THE LAND AND GRAIN.

Very sharp are the excellent shares, With which they set to work on the south-lying, acres.

They sow their various kinds of grain, Each seed containing in it a germ of life.

There are those who come to see them, With their baskets round and square, Containing the provisions of millet.

With their light splint hats on their heads, They ply their hoes on the ground, Clearing away the smartweed on the dry land and wet.

The weeds being decayed, The millets grow luxuriantly.

They fall rustling before the reapers. The gathered crop is piled up solidly, High as a wall, United together like the teeth of a comb; And the hundred houses are opened (to receive the grain)[1].

Those hundred houses being full, The wives and children have a feeling of repose.

(Now) we kill this black-muzzled tawny bull[2], with his crooked horns, To imitate and hand down, To hand down (the observances of) our ancestors.

ODE 7. THE SZE Î.

AN ODE APPROPRIATE TO THE PREPARATIONS AND PROGRESS OF A FEAST AFTER A SACRIFICE.

The Preface and the editors of the Yung-khang Shih say that the piece has reference to the entertainment given, the day after a

1. 'The hundred houses,' or chambers in a hundred family residences, are those of the hundred families, cultivating the space which was bounded by a brook;—see note on the second ode of the preceding decade. They formed a society, whose members helped one another in their field work, so that their harvest might be said to be carried home at the same time. Then would come the threshing or treading, and winnowing, after which the groin would be brought into the houses.
2. It has been observed that under the Kâu dynasty, red was the colour of the sacrificial victims. So it was for the ancestral temple but in sacrificing to the spirits of the land and grain, the victim was a 'yellow' bull with black lips.

sacrifice, in the ancestral temple, to the personators of the dead, described on p. 301. Kû Hsî denies this, and holds simply that it belongs to the feast after a sacrifice, without further specifying what sacrifice. The old view is probably the more correct.

In his silken robes, clean and bright, With his cap on his head, looking so respectful, From the hall he goes to the foot of the stairs, And (then) from the sheep to the oxen[1]. (He inspects) the tripods, large and small, And the curved goblet of rhinoceros horn[2]. The good spirits are mild, (But) there is no noise, no insolence:—An auspice (this) of great longevity.

ODE 8. THE KO.

AN ODE IN PRAISE OF KING WÛ, AND RECOGNISING THE DUTY TO FOLLOW HIS COURSE.

This was sung, according to the Preface, at the conclusion of the dance in honour of king Wû;—see on the last piece of the second decade.

Oh! powerful was the king's army, But he nursed it, in obedience to circumstances, while the

1. The subject of these lines must be an ordinary officer, for to such the silk robes and a purple cap were proper, when he was assisting at the sacrifices of the king or of a feudal prince. There were two buildings outside the principal gate leading to the ancestral temple, and two corresponding inside, in which the personators of the departed ancestors were feasted. We must suppose the officer in question descending from the upper hall to the vestibule of the gate, to inspect the dishes, arranged for the feast, and then proceeding to see the animals, and the tripods for boiling the flesh, &c.
2. The goblet of rhinoceros horn was to be drained, as a penalty, by any one offending at the feast against the rules of propriety; but here there was no occasion for it

time was yet dark. When the time was clearly bright, He thereupon donned his grand armour. We have been favoured to receive What the martial king accomplished. To deal aright with what we have inherited, We have to be sincere imitators of thy course, (O king).

ODE 9. THE HWAN.

CELEBRATING THE MERIT AND SUCCESS OF KING WÛ.

According to a statement in the Zo Kwan, this piece also was sung in connexion with the dance of Wû. The Preface says it was used in declarations of war, and in sacrificing to God and the Father of War. Perhaps it came to be used on such occasions; but we must refer it in the first place to the reign of king Khang.

There is peace throughout our myriad regions. There has been a succession of plentiful years:—Heaven does not weary in its favour. The martial king Wû Maintained (the confidence of) his officers, And employed them all over the kingdom, So securing the establishment of his family. Oh! glorious was he in the sight of Heaven, Which kinged him in the room (of Shang).

ODE 10. THE LÂI.

CELEBRATING THE PRAISE OF KING WAN.

This is the only account of the piece that can be given from itself. The Zo Kwan, however, refers it to the dance of king Wû; and the Preface says it contains the words with which Wû accompanied his grant of fiefs and appanages in the ancestral temple to his principal followers.

King Wan laboured earnestly:—Right is it we should have received (the kingdom). We will diffuse (his virtue), ever cherishing the thought of him; Henceforth we will seek only the settlement (of the kingdom). It was he through whom came the appointment of Kâu. Oh! let us ever cherish the thought of him.

ODE 11. THE PAN.

CELEBRATING THE GREATNESS OF KÂU, AND ITS FIRM POSSESSION OF THE KINGDOM, AS SEEN IN THE PROGRESSES OF ITS REIGNING SOVEREIGN.

In the eighth piece of the first decade we have an ode akin to this, relating a tentative progress of king Wû, to test the acceptance of his sovereignty. This is of a later date, and should be referred, probably, to the reign of king Khang, when the dynasty was fully acknowledged. Some critics, however, make it, like the three preceding, a portion of what was sung at the Wû dance.

Oh! great now is Kâu. We ascend the high hills, Both those that are long and narrow, and the lofty mountains. Yes, and (we travel) along the regulated Ho, All under the sky, Assembling those who now respond to me. Thus it is that the appointment belongs to Kâu.

III. THE PRAISE ODES OF LÛ.

IT is not according to the truth of things to class the Sung of Lû among the sacrificial odes, and I do not call them such. Kû Hsî says:—'King Khang, because of the great services rendered by the duke of Kâu, granted to Po-khin, (the duke's eldest son, and first marquis of Lû), the privilege of using the royal ceremonies and music, in consequence of which Lû had its Sung, which were sung to the music in its ancestral temple. Afterwards, they made in Lû other odes in praise of their rulers, which they also called Sung.' In this way it is endeavoured to account for there being such pieces in this part of the Shih as the four in this division of it. Confucius, it is thought, found them in Lû, bearing the name of Sung, and so he classed them with the true sacrificial odes, bearing that designation. If we were to admit, contrary to the evidence in the case, that the Shih was compiled by Confucius, this explanation of the place, of the Sung of Lû in this Part would not be complimentary to his discrimination.

Whether such a privilege as Kû states was really granted to the first marquis of Lû, is a point very much controverted. Many contend that the royal ceremonies were usurped in the state,—in the time of duke Hsî (B.C. 659 to 627). But if this should be conceded, it would not affect the application to the odes in this division of the name of Sung. They are totally unlike the Sung of Shang and of Kâu. It has often been asked why there are no Fang of Lû in the first Part of the Shih. The pieces here are really the Fang of Lû, and may be compared especially with the Fang of Pin.

Lû was one of the states in the east, having its capital in Khü-fâu, which is still the name of a district in the department of Yen-kâu, Shan-tung. According to Kû, king Khang invested the duke of Kâu's eldest son with the territory. According to Sze-ma Khien, the duke of Kâu was himself appointed marquis of Lû; but being unable to go there in consequence of his duties at the royal court, he sent his son instead. After the expiration of his 'regency, the territory was largely augmented, but he still remained in Kâu.

I pass over the first two odes, which have no claim to a place among 'sacred texts.' And only in one stanza of the third is there the expression of a religious sentiment. I give it entire, however.

ODE 3. THE PHAN SHUI.

IN PRAISE OF SOME MARQUIS OF LÛ, CELEBRATING HIS INTEREST IN THE STATE COLLEGE, WHICH HE HAD, PROBABLY, REPAIRED, TESTIFYING HIS VIRTUES, AND AUSPICING FOR HIM A COMPLETE TRIUMPH OVER THE TRIBES OF THE HWÂI, WHICH WOULD BE CELEBRATED IN THE COLLEGE.

The marquis here celebrated was, probably, Shan, or 'duke Hsî,' mentioned above. The immediate occasion of its composition must have been some opening or inauguration service in connexion with the repair of the college.

1. Pleasant is the semicircular water [1], And we gather the cress about it. The marquis of Lû is coming to it, And we see his dragon-figured banner. His banner waves in the wind, And the bells of his horses tinkle harmoniously. Small and great, All follow the prince in his progress to it.

2. Pleasant is the semicircular water, And we gather the pondweed in it. The marquis of Lû has come to it, With his horses so stately. His horses are grand; His fame is brilliant. Blandly he looks and smiles; Without any impatience he delivers his instructions.
3. Pleasant is the semicircular water, And we gather the mallows about it. The marquis of Lû has come to it, And in the college he is drinking. He is drinking the good spirits. May there be

1. It is said in the tenth ode of the first decade of the Major Odes of the Kingdom, that king Wû in his capital of Hâo built 'his hall with its circlet of water.' That was the royal college built in the middle of a circle of water; each state had its grand college with a semicircular pool in front of it, such is may now be seen in front of the temples of Confucius in the metropolitan cities of the provinces. It is not easy to describe all the purposes which the building served. In this piece the marquis of Lû appears feasting in it, delivering instructions, taking counsel with his ministers, and receiving the spoils and prisoners of war. The Lî Kî, VIII, ii, 7, refers to sacrifices to Hâu kî in connexion with the college of Lû. There the officers of the state in autumn learned ceremonies; in winter, literary studies; in spring and summer, the use of arms; and in autumn and winter, dancing. There were celebrated trials of archery; there the aged were feasted; there the princes held council with their ministers. The college was in the western suburb of each capital.

given to him such old age as is seldom enjoyed! May he accord with the grand ways, So subduing to himself all the people!

4. Very admirable is the marquis of Lû, Reverently displaying his virtue, And reverently watching over his deportment, The pattern of the people.

    With great qualities, both civil and martial, Brilliantly he affects his meritorious ancestors [1]. In everything entirely filial, He seeks the blessing that is sure to follow.
5. Very intelligent is the marquis of Lû, Making his virtue illustrious. He has made this college with its semicircle of water, And the tribes of the Hwâi will submit to him [2]. His martial-looking tiger-leaders Will here present the left ears (of their foes) [3]. His examiners, wise as Kâo-yâo [4] Will here present the prisoners.
6. His numerous officers, Men who have enlarged their virtuous minds, With martial energy conducting their expedition, Will

drive far away those tribes of the east and south. Vigorous and

1. The meaning is that the fine qualities of the marquis 'reached to' and affected his ancestors in their spirit-state, and would draw down their protecting favour. Their blessing, seen in his prosperity, was the natural result of his filial piety.
2. The Hwâi rises in the department of Nan-yang, Ho-nan, and flows eastward to the sea. South of it, down to the time of this ode, were many rude and wild tribes that gave frequent occupation to the kings of Kâu.
3. When prisoners refused to submit, their left ears were cut off, and shown as trophies.
4. The ancient Shun's Minister of Crime. The 'examiners' were officers. who questioned the prisoners, especially the more important of them, to elicit information, and decide as to the amount of their guilt and punishment.

grand, Without noise or display, Without appeal to the judges [1], They will here present (the proofs of) their merit.

7. How they draw their bows adorned with bone! How their arrows whiz forth! Their war chariots are very large! Their footmen and charioteers never weary! They have subdued the tribes of Hwâi, And brought them to an unrebellious submission. Only lay your plans securely, And all the tribes of the Hwâi will be won [2].
8. They come flying on the wing, those owls, And settle on the trees about the college; They eat the fruit of our mulberry trees, And salute us with fine notes [3]. So awakened shall be those tribes of the Hwâi. They will come presenting their precious things, Their large tortoises, and their elephants' teeth, And great contributions of the southern metals [4].

1. The 'judges' decided all questions of dispute in the army, and on the merits of different men who had distinguished themselves.
2. In this stanza the poet describes a battle with the wild tribes, as if it were going on before his eyes.
3 An owl is a bird with a disagreeable scream, instead of a beautiful note; but the mulberries grown about the college would make them sing delightfully. And so would the influence of Lû, going forth from the college, transform the nature of the tribes about the Hwâi.
4 That is, according to 'the Tribute of Yü,' in the Shû, from King-kâu and Yang-kâu.

ODE 4. THE PÎ KUNG.

IN PRAISE OF DUKE HSÎ, AND AUSPICING FOR HIM A MAGNIFICENT CAREER OF SUCCESS, WHICH WOULD MAKE-LÛ ALL THAT IT HAD EVER BEEN:—WRITTEN, PROBABLY, ON AN OCCASION WHEN HSÎ HAD REPAIRED THE TEMPLES OF THE STATE, OF WHICH PIOUS ACT HIS SUCCESS WOULD BE THE REWARD.

There is no doubt that duke Hsî is the hero of this piece. He is mentioned in the third stanza as 'the son of duke Kwang,' and the Hsî-sze referred to in the last stanza as the architect under whose superintendence the temples had been repaired was his brother, whom we meet with elsewhere as 'duke's son, Yü'. The descriptions of various sacrifices prove that the lords of Lû, whether permitted to use royal ceremonies or not, did really do so. The writer was evidently in a poetic rapture as to what his ruler was, and would do. The piece is a genuine bardic effusion.

The poet traces the lords of Lû to Khang Yüen and her son Hâu-kî. He then comes to the establishment of the Kâu dynasty, and under it of the marquisate of Lû; and finally to duke Hsî, dilating on his sacrificial services, the military power of Lû, and the achievements which be might be expected to accomplish in subjugating all the territory lying to the east and a long way South, of Lû.

I. How pure and still are the solemn temples, In their strong solidity and minute completeness! Highly distinguished was Kiang Yüan[1], Of virtue undeflected. God regarded her with favour, And without injury or hurt, Immediately, when her months were completed, She gave birth to Hâu-kî! On him were conferred all blessings,— (To know) how the (ordinary) millet ripened early, and the sacrificial millet late; How first to sow pulse

1. About Kiang Yüan and her conception and birth of Hâu-kî, see the first piece in the third decade of the Major Odes of the Kingdom. There also Hâu-kî's teaching of husbandry is more fully described.

and then wheat. Anon he was invested with an inferior state, And taught the people how to sow and to reap, The (ordinary) millet and the sacrificial, Rice and the black millet; Ere long over the whole country:—(Thus) continuing the work of Yü.

2. Among the descendants of Hâu-kî, There was king Thâi[1], Dwelling on the south of (mount) Khî, Where the clipping of Shang began. In process of time Wan and Wû Continued the work of king Thâi, And (the purpose of) Heaven was carried out in its time, In the plain of Mû [2]. 'Have no doubts, no anxieties,'—(it was said), 'God is with you [3].' Wû disposed of the troops of Shang; He and his men equally, shared in the achievement. (Then) king (Khang) said, 'My uncle [4], I will set up your eldest son, And make him marquis of Lû. I will greatly enlarge your territory there, To be a help and support to the House of Kâu.'

3. Accordingly he appointed (our first) duke of Lo, And made him marquis in the east, Giving him the hills and rivers, The lands and fields, and the attached states [5]. The (present) descendant of the duke of Kâu, The son of duke Kwang, With dragon-emblazoned banner, attends the sacrifices, (Grasping) his six reins soft and pliant. In spring

1. See on the Sacrificial Odes of Kâu, decade i, ode 5.
2. See the Shû, V, iii.
3. Shang-fû, one of Wû's principal leaders, encouraged him at the battle of Mû with these words.
4 That is, the duke of Kâu.
5 That is, small territories, held by chiefs of other surnames, but acknowledging the jurisdiction of. the lords of Lû, and dependent on them for introduction to the royal court.

and autumn he is not remiss; His offerings are all without error[1]. To the great and sovereign God, And to his great ancestor Hâu-kî, He offers the victims, red and pure [2] They enjoy, they approve, And bestow blessings in large number. The duke of Kâu, and (your other) great ancestors, Also bless you.

4. In autumn comes the sacrifice of the season[3], But the bulls for it have had their horns capped in summer [4]; They are the white bull and the red one [5]. (There are) the bull-figured goblet in, its dignity [6]; Roast pig, minced meat, and soups; The dishes of bamboo and wood, and the large stands [7], And the dancers all complete. The filial descendant

1. These lines refer to the seasonal sacrifices in the temple of ancestors, two seasons being mentioned for all the four, as in some of the odes of Shang.
2. From the seasonal sacrifices the poet passes to the sacrifice to God at the border altar in the spring,—no doubt the same which is referred to in the last ode of the first decade of the Sacrificial Odes of Kâu.
3. The subject of the seasonal sacrifices is resumed.
4. A piece of wood was fixed across the horns of the victim-bulls, to prevent their injuring them by pushing or rubbing against any hard substance. An animal injured in any way was not fit to be used in sacrifice.
5. In sacrificing to the duke of Kâu, a white bull was used by way of distinction. His great services to the. dynasty had obtained for him the privilege of being sacrificed to with royal ceremonies. A white bull, such as had been offered to the kings of Shang, was therefore devoted to him; while for Po-khin, and 'the other marquises (or dukes as spoken of by their own subjects), a victim of the orthodox Kâu colour was employed.
6. This goblet, fashioned in the shape of a bull, or with a bull pictured on it, must have been well known in connexion with these services.
7. 'The large stand' was of a size to support half the roasted body of a victim.

will be blessed. (Your ancestors) will make you gloriously prosperous, They will make you long-lived and good, To preserve this eastern, region, Long possessing the state of Lû, Unwaning, unfallen, Unshaken, undisturbed! They will make your friendship with your three aged (ministers)[1] Like the hills, like the mountains.

5. Our prince's chariots are a thousand, And (in each) are (the two spears with their) vermilion tassels, and (the two bows with their) green bands. His footmen are thirty thousand, With shells on vermilion strings adorning their helmets [2]. So numerous are his ardent followers, To deal with the tribes of the west and north, And to punish those of King and Shû [3], So that none of them will dare to withstand us. (The spirits of your ancestors) shall make you grandly prosperous; They

1. Referring, probably, to the three principal ministers of the state.
2. These lines describe Hsî's resources for war. A thousand chariots was the regular force which a great state could at the utmost bring into the field. Each chariot contained three mailed men; the charioteer in the middle, a spearman on the right, and an archer on the left. Two spears rose aloft with vermilion tassels, and there were two bows, bound with green bands to frames in their cases. Attached to every chariot were seventy-two foot-soldiers and twenty-five followers, making with the three men in it, 100 in all; so that the whole force would amount to 100,000 men. But in actual service the force of a great state was restricted to three 'armies' or 375 chariots, attended by 37,500 men, of whom 27,500 were foot-soldiers, put down here in round numbers as 30,000.

3. King is the King-khû of the last of the Sacrificial Odes of Shang, and the name Shû was applied to several half-civilized states to the east of it, which it brought, during the Khun Khiû period, one after another under its jurisdiction.

shall make you long-lived and wealthy. The hoary hair and wrinkled back, Marking the aged men, shall always be in your service. They shall grant you old age, ever vigorous, For myriads and thousands of years, With the eyebrows of longevity, and ever unharmed.

6. The mountain of Thâi is lofty, Looked up to by the state of Lû [1]. We grandly possess also Kwei and Mang [2]. And we shall extend to the limits of the east, Even the states along the sea. The tribes of the Hwâi will seek our alliance; All will proffer their allegiance:—Such shall be the achievements of the marquis of Lû.

7. He shall maintain the possession of Hû and Yî [3], And extend his sway to the regions of Hsü [4], Even to the states along the sea. The tribes of the Hwâi, the Man, and the Mo [5], And those tribes (still more) to the south, All will proffer their allegiance;—Not one will dare not to answer to his call, Thus showing their obedience to the marquis of Lû.

8. Heaven will give great blessing to our prince, So that with the eyebrows of longevity he shall

1. Mount Thâi is well known, the eastern of the four great mountains of China in the time of Shun. It is in the department of Thâi-an, Shan-tung.
2. These were two smaller hills in Lû.
3. These were two hills of Lû, in the present district of Zâu.
4. Hsü was the name of one of Yü's nine provinces, embracing portions of the present Shan-tung, Kiang-sû, and An-hui.
5. Mo was properly the name of certain wild tribes in the north, as Man was that of the tribes of the south. But we cannot suppose any tribes to be meant here but such as lay south of Lû.

maintain Lû. He shall possess Kang and Hsü[1], And recover all the territory of the duke of Kâu. Then shall the marquis of Lû feast and be glad, With his admirable wife and aged mother; With his excellent ministers and all his (other) officers[2]. Our region and state shall he hold, Thus receiving many blessings, To hoary hair, and with teeth ever renewed like a child's.

9. The pines of Zû-lâi [3], And the cypresses of Hsin-fû [3], Were cut down and measured, With the cubit line and the eight cubits' line. The projecting beams of pine were made very large; The grand inner apartments rose vast. Splendid look the new

temples, The work of Hsî-sze, Very wide and large, Answering to the expectations of all the people.

1. Kang was a city with some adjacent territory, in the present district of Thang, that had been taken from Lû by Khî. Hsü, called in the Spring and Autumn 'the fields of Hsü' was west from Lû, and had been granted to it as a convenient place for its princes to stop at on their way to the royal court; but it had been sold or parted with to Kang in the first year of duke Hwan (B.C. 711). The poet desires that Hsî should recover these and all other territory which had at any time belonged to Lû.
2. He would feast with the ladies in the inner apartment of the palace, suitable for such a purpose; with his ministers in the outer banqueting-room.
3. These were two hills, in the present department of Thâi-an.

II.

THE MINOR ODES OF THE KINGDOM.

PIECES AND STANZAS ILLUSTRATING THE RELIGIOUS VIEWS AND PRACTICES OF THE WRITERS AND THEIR TIMES.

The First Decade, or that of Lû-ming.

ODE 5, STANZA 1. THE FÂ MÛ.

THE FÂ MÛ IS A FESTAL ODE, WHICH WAS SUNG AT THE ENTERTAINMENT OF FRIENDS;—INTENDED TO CELEBRATE THE DUTY AND VALUE OF FRIENDSHIP, EVEN TO THE HIGHEST.

On the trees go the blows kang-kang; And the birds cry out ying-ying. One issues from the dark valley, And removes to the lofty tree. Ying goes its cry, Seeking with its voice its companion. Look at the bird, Bird as it is, seeking with its. voice its companion; And shall a man Not seek to have his friends? Spiritual beings will then hearken to him[1]; He shall have harmony and peace.

ODE 6. THE THIEN PÂO.

A FESTAL ODE, RESPONSIVE TO ANY OF THE FIVE THAT PRECEDE IT. THE KING'S OFFICERS AND GUESTS, HAVING BEEN FEASTED BY HIM, CELEBRATE HIS PRAISES, AND DESIRE FOR HIM THE BLESSING OF HEAVEN AND HIS ANCESTORS.

Ascribed, like the former, to the duke of Kâu.

Heaven protects and establishes thee, With the greatest. security; Makes thee entirely virtuous.

1. This line and the following show the power and value of the cultivation of friendship in affecting spiritual beings. That destination is understood in the widest sense.

That thou mayest enjoy every happiness; Grants thee much increase, So that thou hast all in abundance.

Heaven protects and establishes thee. It grants thee all excellence, So that thine every matter is right, And thou receivest every Heavenly favour. It sends down to thee long-during happiness, Which the days are not sufficient to enjoy.

Heaven protects and establishes thee, So that in everything thou dost prosper. Like the high hills and the mountain masses, Like the topmost ridges and the greatest bulks, Like the stream ever coming on, Such is thine increase.

With happy auspices and purifications thou bringest the offerings, And dost filially present them, In spring, summer, autumn, and winter, To the dukes and former kings[1]; And they say, 'We give to thee myriads of years, duration unlimited [2].'

The spirits come [3], And confer on thee many blessings. The people are simple and honest, Daily enjoying their meat, and drink. All the black-haired race, in all their surnames, Universally practise thy virtue.

Like the moon advancing to the full, Like the sun ascending the heavens, Like the everlasting southern hills, Never waning, never falling, Like

1. These dukes and former kings are all the ancestors of the royal House of Kâu, sacrificed to at the four seasons of the year.
2. Here we have the response of the dukes and kings communicated to the sacrificing king by the individuals chosen to represent them at the service.
3. The spirits here are, of course, those of the former dukes and kings.

the luxuriance of the fir and the cypress;—May such be thy succeeding line!

ODE 9, STANZA 4. THE TÎ TÛ.

THE TÎ TÛ IS AN ODE OF CONGRATULATION, INTENDED FOR THE MEN WHO HAVE RETURNED FROM MILITARY DUTY AND SERVICE ON THE FRONTIERS.

The congratulation is given in a description of the anxiety and longing of the soldiers' wives for their return. We must suppose one of the wives to be the speaker throughout. The fourth stanza shows how she had resorted to divination to allay her fears about her husband.

They have not packed up, they do not come. My sorrowing heart is greatly distressed. The time is past, and he is not here, To the multiplication of my sorrows. Both by the tortoise-shell and the reeds have I divined, And they unite in saying he is near. My warrior is at hand.

The Fourth Decade, or that of Khî fû.

ODE 5, STANZAS 5 TO 9. THE SZE KAN.

THE SZE KAN WAS, PROBABLY MADE FOR A FESTIVAL ON THE COMPLETION OF A PALACE; CONTAINING A DESCRIPTION OF IT, AND PROCEEDING TO GOOD WISHES FOR THE BUILDER AND HIS POSTERITY. THE STANZAS HERE GIVEN SHOW HOW DIVINATION

WAS RESORTED TO FOR THE INTERPRETATION OF DREAMS.

The piece is referred to the time of king Hsüan (B.C. 827 to 782).

Level and smooth is the courtyard, And lofty are the pillars around it. Pleasant is the exposure of the chamber to the light, And deep and wide are its recesses. Here will our noble lord repose.

On the rush-mat below and that of fine bamboos above it, May he repose in slumber! May he sleep and awake, (Saying), 'Divine for me my dreams[1]. What dreams are lucky? They have been of bears and grisly bears; They have been of cobras and (other) snakes.'

The chief diviner will divine them. 'The bears and grisly bears Are the auspicious intimations of sons; The cobras and (other) snakes Are the auspicious intimations of daughters[2].'

Sons shall be born to him:—They will be put to sleep on couches; They will be clothed in robes; They will have sceptres to play with; Their cry will be loud. They will be (hereafter) resplendent with red knee-covers, The (future) king, the princes of the land.

Daughters shall be born to him:-They will be put to sleep on the ground; They will be clothed with wrappers; They will have tiles to play with[3]. It will be theirs neither to do wrong nor to do good[4]. Only about the spirits and the food will

1. In the Official Book of Kâu, ch. 24, mention is made of the Diviner of Dreams and his duties:—He had to consider the season of the year when a dream occurred, the day of the cycle, and the then predominant influence of the two powers of nature. By the positions of the sun, moon, and planets in the zodiacal spaces he could determine whether any one of the six classes of dreams was lucky or unlucky. Those six classes were ordinary and regular dreams, terrible dreams, dreams of thought, dreams in waking, dreams of joy, and dreams of fear.
2. The boy would have a sceptre, a symbol of dignity, to play with; the girl, a tile, the symbol of woman's work, as, sitting with a tile on her knee, she twists the threads of hemp.
3. That is, the red apron of a king and of the prince of a state.
4. The woman has only to be obedient. That is her whole duty. The line does not mean, as it has been said, that 'she is incapable of good or evil;' but it is not her part to take the initiative even in what is good.

they have to think, And to cause no sorrow to their parents.

ODE 6, STANZA 4. THE WÛ YANG.

THE WÛ YANG IS SUPPOSED TO CELEBRATE THE LARGENESS AND EXCELLENT CONDITION OF KING HSÜAN'S FLOCKS AND HERDS. THE CONCLUDING STANZA HAS REFERENCE TO THE DIVINATION OF THE DREAMS OF HIS HERDSMEN.

Your herdsmen shall dream, Of multitudes and then of fishes, Of the tortoise-and-serpent, and then of the falcon, banners[1]. The chief diviner will. divine the dreams;—How the multitudes, dissolving into fishes, Betoken plentiful years; How the tortoise-and-serpent, dissolving into the falcon, banners, Betoken the increasing population of the kingdom.

ODE 7. THE KIEH NAN SHAN.

A LAMENTATION OVER THE UNSETTLED STATE OF THE KINGDOM DENOUNCING THE INJUSTICE AND NEGLECT OF THE CHIEF MINISTER, BLAMING ALSO THE CONDUCT OF THE KING, WITH APPEALS TO HEAVEN, AND SEEMINGLY CHARGING IT WITH CRUELTY AND INJUSTICE.

This piece is referred to-the time of king Yû (B.C. 781, to 771), the unworthy son of king Hsüan. The 'Grand-Master' Yin must have been one of the 'three Kung,' the highest ministers at the court of Kâu, and was, probably, the chief of the three, and administrator of the government under Yû.

Lofty is that southern hill [2], With its masses of rocks! Awe-inspiring are you, O (Grand-)Master

---

1. The tortoise-and-serpent banner marked the presence in a host of its leader on a military expedition. On its field were the figures of tortoises, with snakes coiled round them. The falcon banners belonged to the commanders of the divisions of the host. They bore the figures of falcons on them.
2. 'The southern hill' was also called the Kung-nan, and rose right to the south of the western capital of Kâu.

Yin, And the people all look to you! A fire burns in their grieving hearts; They do not dare to speak of you even in jest. The kingdom is verging to extinction;—How is it that you do not consider the state of things?

Lofty is that southern hill, And vigorously grows the vegetation on it! Awe-inspiring are you,-O (Grand-)Master Yin, But how is it that you are so unjust? Heaven is continually redoubling its inflictions; Deaths and disorder increase and multiply; No words of satisfaction come from the people; And yet you do not correct nor bemoan yourself

The Grand-Master Yin Is the foundation of our Kâu, And the balance of the kingdom is in his hands. He should be keeping its four quarters together; He should be aiding the Son of Heaven, So as to preserve the people from going astray. O unpitying great Heaven, It is not right he should reduce us all to such misery!

He does nothing himself personally, And the people have no confidence in him. Making no enquiry about them, and no trial of their services, He should not deal deceitfully with superior men. If he dismissed them on the requirement of justice, Mean men would not be endangering (the commonweal); And his mean relatives Would not be in offices of importance.

Great Heaven, unjust, Is sending down these exhausting disorders. Great Heaven, unkind, Is sending down these great miseries. Let superior men come (into office), And that would bring rest to the people's hearts. Let superior men execute their justice, And the animosities and angers would disappear[1].

O unpitying great Heaven, There is no end to the disorder! With every month it continues to grow, So that the people have no repose. I am as if intoxicated with the grief of my heart. Who holds the ordering of the kingdom? He attends not himself to the government, And the result is toil and pain to the people.

I yoke my four steeds, My four steeds, long-necked. I look to the four quarters (of the kingdom); Distress is everywhere; there is no place I can drive to.

Now your evil is rampant [2], And I can see your spears. Anon you are pacified and friendly as if you were pledging one another.

From great Heaven is the injustice, And our king has no repose. (Yet) he will not correct his heart, And goes on to resent endeavours to rectify him,

I, Kiâ-fû, have made this poem, To lay bare a the king's disorders. If you would but change your heart, Then would the myriad regions be nourished.

1. In this stanza, as in the next and the last but one, the writer complains of Heaven, and charges it foolishly. He does so by way of appeal, however, and indicates the true causes of the misery of the kingdom,—the reckless conduct, namely, of the king and his minister.
2. The parties spoken of here are the followers of the minister, 'mean men,' however high in place and great in power, now friendly, now hostile to one another.

ODE 8, STANZAS 4, 5, AND 7. THE KANG YÜEH.

THE KANG YÜEH IS, LIKE THE PRECEDING ODE, A LAMENTATION OVER THE MISERIES OF THE KINGDOM, AND THE RUIN COMING ON IT; WITH A SIMILAR, BUT MORE HOPEFULLY EXPRESSED, APPEAL TO HEAVEN, 'THE GREAT GOD.'

Look into the middle of the forest; There are (only) large faggots and small branches in it [1]. The people now amidst their perils Look to Heaven, all dark; But let its determination be fixed, And there is no one whom it will not overcome. There is the great God,—Does he hate any one?

If one say of a hill that it is low, There are its ridges and its large masses. The false calumnies of the people,—How is it that you do not repress them [2]? You call those experienced ancients, You consult the diviner of dreams. They all say, 'We are very wise, But who can distinguish the male and female crow[3]?'

Look at the rugged and stony field;—Luxuriantly rises in it the springing grain. (But) Heaven moves and shakes me, As if it could not overcome me [4].

1. By introducing the word 'only,' I have followed the view of the older interpreters, who consider the forest, with merely some faggots and twigs left in it, to be emblematic of the ravages of oppressive government in the court and kingdom. Ka Hsî takes a different view of them:—'In a forest you can easily distinguish the large faggots from the small branches, while Heaven appears unable to distinguish between the good and bad.'
2. The calumnies that were abroad were as absurd as the assertion in line 1, and yet the king could not, or would not, see through them and repress them.

3. This reference to the diviners of dreams is in derision of their pretensions.
4. That is, the productive energy of nature manifests itself in the most unlikely places; how was it that 'the great God, who hates no one,' was contending so with the writer?

They sought me (at first) to be a pattern (to them), (Eagerly) as if they could not get me; (Now) they regard me with great animosity, And will not use my strength.

ODE 9. THE SHIH YÜEH KIH KIÂO.

THE LAMENTATION OF AN OFFICER OVER THE PRODIGIES CELESTIAL AND TERRESTRIAL, ESPECIALLY AN ECLIPSE OF THE SUN, THAT WERE BETOKENING THE RUIN OF KÂU. HE SETS FORTH WHAT HE CONSIDERED TO BE THE TRUE CAUSES OF THE PREVAILING MISERY, WHICH WAS BY NO MEANS TO BE CHARGED ON HEAVEN.

Attention is called in the Introduction, p. 296, to the date of the solar eclipse mentioned in this piece.

At the conjunction (of the sun and moon) in the tenth month, On the first day of the moon, which was hsin-mâo, The sun was eclipsed, A thing of very evil omen. Before, the moon became small, And now the sun became small. Henceforth the lower people Will be in a very deplorable case.

The sun and moon announce evil, Not keeping to their proper paths. Throughout the kingdom there is no (proper) government, Because the good are not employed. For the moon to be eclipsed Is but an ordinary matter. Now that the sun has been eclipsed,—How bad it is!

Grandly flashes the lightning of the thunder. There is a want of rest, a want of good. The streams all bubble up and overflow. The crags on the hill-tops fall down. High banks become valleys; Deep valleys become hills. Alas for the men of this time! How does (the king) not stop these things?

Hwang-fû is the President; Fan is the Minister of Instruction; Kiâ-po is the (chief) Administrator; Kung-yün is the chief Cook;

Zâu is the Recorder of the Interior; Khwei is Master of the Horse; Yü is Captain of the Guards; And the beautiful wife blazes, now in possession of her place [1].

This Hwang-fû Will not acknowledge that he is acting. out of season. But why does he call us to move, Without coming and consulting with us? He has removed our walls and roofs; And our fields are all either a marsh or a moor. He says, 'I am not injuring you; The laws require that thus it should be.'

Hwang-fû is very wise; He has built a great city for himself in Hsiang. He chose three men as his ministers, All of them possessed of great wealth. He could not bring himself to leave a single minister, Who might guard our king. He (also) selected those who had chariots and horses, To go and reside in Hsiang [2].

1. We do not know anything from history of the ministers of Yû mentioned in this stanza. Hwang-fû appears to have been the leading minister of the government at the time when the ode was written, and, as appears from the next two stanzas, was very crafty, oppressive, and selfishly ambitious. The mention of 'the chief Cook' among the high ministers appears strange; but we shall find that functionary mentioned in another ode; and from history it appears that 'the Cook,' at the royal and feudal courts, sometimes played an important part during the times of Kâu. 'The beautiful wife,' no doubt, was the well-known Sze of Pâo, raised by king Yû from her position as one of his concubines to be his queen, and whose insane folly and ambition led to her husband's death, and great and disastrous changes in the kingdom.
2. Hsiang was a district of the royal domain, in the present district of Mang, department of Hwâi-khing, Ho-nan. It had been assigned to Hwang-fû, and he was establishing himself there, without any loyal regard to the king. As a noble in the royal domain, he was entitled only to two ministers, but he had appointed three as in one of the feudal states, encouraging, moreover, the resort to himself of the wealthy and powerful, while the court was left weak and unprotected.

I have exerted myself to discharge my service, And do not dare to make a report of my toils. Without crime or offence of any kind, Slanderous mouths are loud against me. (But) the calamities of the lower people Do not come down from Heaven. A multitude of (fair) words, and hatred behind the back;—The earnest, strong pursuit of this is from men.

Distant far is my village, And my dissatisfaction is great. In other quarters there is ease, And I dwell here, alone and sorrowful. Everybody is going into retirement, And I alone dare not seek rest. The ordinances of Heaven are inexplicable, But I will not dare to follow my friends, and leave my post.

ODE 10, STANZAS I AND 3. THE YÜ WÛ KANG.

THE WRITER OF THIS PIECE MOURNS OVER THE MISERABLE STATE OF THE KINGDOM, THE INCORRIGIBLE COURSE OF THE KING, AND OTHER EVILS, APPEALING ALSO TO HEAVEN, AND SURPRISED THAT IT ALLOWED SUCH THINGS TO BE.

Great and wide Heaven, How is it you have contracted your kindness, Sending down death and famine, Destroying all through the kingdom? Compassionate Heaven, arrayed in terrors, How is it you exercise no forethought, no care? Let alone the criminals:—They have suffered for their guilt. But those who have no crime Are indiscriminately involved in ruin.

How is it, O great Heaven, That the king will not hearken to the justest words? He is like a man going (astray), Who knows not where he will proceed to. All ye officers, Let each of you attend to his duties. How do ye not stand in awe of one another? Ye do not stand in awe of Heaven.

The Fifth Decade, or that of Hsiâo Min.

ODE 1, STANZAS 1, 2, AND 3. THE HSIÂO MIN.

A LAMENTATION OVER THE RECKLESSNESS AND INCAPACITY OF THE KING AND HIS COUNSELLORS. DIVINATION HAS BECOME OF NO AVAIL, AND HEAVEN IS DESPAIRINGLY APPEALED TO.

This is referred, like several of the pieces in the fourth decade, to the time of king Yû.

The angry terrors of compassionate Heaven Extend through this lower world. (The king's) counsels and plans are crooked and bad; When will he stop (in his course)? Counsels that are good he will not follow, And those that are not good he employs. When I look at his counsels and plans, I am greatly pained.

Now they agree, and now they defame one another;—The case is greatly to be deplored. If a counsel be good, They are all found opposing it. If a counsel be bad, They are all found according with it. When I look at such counsels and plans, What will they come to?

Our tortoise-shells are wearied out, And will not tell us anything about the plans. The counsellors are very many, But on that account nothing is accomplished. The speakers fill the court, But who dares to take any responsibility on himself? We are as if we consulted (about a journey) without taking a step in advance, And therefore did not get on on the road.

ODE 2, STANZAS I AND 2. THE HSIÂO YÜAN.

SOME OFFICER IN A TIME OF DISORDER AND MISGOVERNMENT URGES ON HIS BROTHERS THE DUTY OF MAINTAINING THEIR OWN VIRTUE, AND OF OBSERVING THE GREATEST CAUTION.

Small is the cooing dove, But it flies aloft to heaven. My heart is wounded with sorrow, And I think of our forefathers. When the dawn is breaking, and I cannot sleep, The thoughts in my breast are of our parents.

Men who are grave and wise, Though they drink, are mild and masters of themselves; But those who are benighted and ignorant Become devoted to drink, and more so daily. Be careful, each of you, of your deportment; What Heaven confers, (when once lost), is not regained[1].

The greenbeaks come and go, Picking up grain about the stackyard. Alas for the distressed and the solitary, Deemed fit inmates for the prisons! With a handful of grain I go out and divine[2], How I may be able to become good.

1. 'What Heaven confers' is, probably, the good human nature which by vice, and especially by drunkenness, may be irretrievably ruined.
2. A religious act is here referred to, on which we have not sufficient information to be able to throw much light. It was the practice to spread some finely ground rice on the ground, in connexion with divination, as an offering to the spirits. The poet

represents himself here as using a handful of grain for the purpose,—probably on account of his poverty.

ODE 3, STANZAS 1 AND 3. THE HSIÂO PAN.

THE ELDEST SON AND HEIR-APPARENT OF KING YÛ BEWAILS HIS DEGRADATION, APPEALING TO HEAVEN AS TO HIS INNOCENCE, AND COMPLAINING OF ITS CASTING HIS LOT IN SUCH A TIME.

It is allowed that this piece is clearly the composition of a banished son, and there is no necessity to call in question the tradition preserved in the Preface which prefers it to Î-khiû, the eldest son of king Yû. His mother was a princess of the House of Shan, but when Yü became enamoured of Sze of Pâo, the queen was degraded, and the son banished to Shan.

With flapping wings the crows Come back, flying all in a flock[1]. Other people are happy, And I only am full of misery. What is my offence against Heaven? What is my crime? My heart is sad; What is to be done?

Even the mulberry trees and the rottleras Must be regarded with reverence [2]; But no one is to be looked up to like a father, No one is to be depended on as a mother. Have I not a connexion with the hairs (of my father)? Did I not dwell in the womb (of my mother)? O Heaven, who gave me birth! How was it at so inauspicious a time?

1. The sight of the crows, all together, suggests to the prince his own condition, solitary and driven from court.
2. The mulberry tree and the rottlera were both planted about the farmsteadings, and are therefore mentioned here. They carried the thoughts back to the father or grandfather, or the more remote ancestor, who first planted them, and so a feeling of reverence attached to themselves.

ODE 4, STANZA 1. THE KHIÂO YEN.

SOME ONE, SUFFERING FROM THE KING THROUGH SLANDER, APPEALS TO HEAVEN, AND GOES ON TO DWELL ON THE NATURE AND EVIL OF SLANDER.

This piece has been referred to the time of king Lî, B.C. 878 to 828.

O vast and distant Heaven, Who art called our parent, That, without crime or offence, I should suffer from disorders thus great! The terrors of great Heaven are excessive, But indeed I have committed no crime. (The terrors. of) great Heaven are very excessive, But indeed I have committed no offence.

ODE 6, STANZAS 5 AND 6. THE HSIANG PO.

A EUNUCH, HIMSELF THE VICTIM OF SLANDER, COMPLAINS OF HIS FATE, AND WARNS AND DENOUNCES HIS ENEMIES; APPEALING AGAINST THEM, AS HIS LAST RESORT, TO HEAVEN.

The proud are delighted, And the troubled are in sorrow. O azure Heaven! O azure Heaven! Look on those proud men, Pity those who are troubled.

Those slanderers! Who devised their schemes for them? I would take those slanderers, And throw them to wolves and tigers. If these refused to devour them, I would cast them into the north[1]. If the north refused to receive them, I would throw them into the hands of great (Heaven) [2].

---

1. 'The north,' i.e. the region where there are the rigours of winter and the barrenness of the desert.
2. 'Great Heaven;' 'Heaven' has to be supplied here, but there is no doubt as to the propriety of doing so; and, moreover, the peculiar phraseology of the line shows that the poet did not rest in the thought of the material heavens.

ODE 9. THE TÂ TUNG.

AN OFFICER OF ONE OF THE STATES OF THE EAST DEPLORES THE EXACTIONS MADE FROM THEM BY THE GOVERNMENT, COMPLAINS OF THE FAVOUR SHOWN TO THE WEST, CONTRASTS THE MISERY OF THE PRESENT WITH THE HAPPINESS OF THE PAST, AND APPEALS TO THE STARS OF HEAVEN IDLY BEHOLDING THEIR CONDITION.

I give the whole of this piece, because it is an interesting instance of Sabian views. The writer, despairing of help from men, appeals to Heaven; but he distributes the Power that could help him among many heavenly bodies, supposing that there are spiritual beings in them, taking account of human affairs.

Well loaded with millet were the dishes, And long and curved were the spoons of thorn-wood. The way to Kâu was like a whetstone, And straight as an arrow. (So) the officers trod it, And the common people looked on it. When I look back and think of it, My tears run down in streams.

In the states of the east, large and small, The looms are empty. Then shoes of dolichos fibre Are made to serve to walk on the hoar-frost. Slight and elegant gentlemen[1] Walk along that road to Kâu. Their going and coming makes my heart sad.

Ye cold waters, issuing variously from the spring, Do not soak the firewood I have cut. Sorrowful, I awake and sigh;—Alas for us toiled people! The firewood has been cut;—Would that it were

---

1. That is, 'slight-looking,' unfit for toil; and yet they are obliged to make their journey on foot.

---

conveyed home! Alas for us the toiled people! Would that we could have rest[1]!

The sons of the east Are summoned only (to service), without encouragement; While the sons of the west Shine in splendid dresses. The sons of boatmen Have furs of the bear and grisly bear. The sons of the poorest families Form the officers in public employment.

If we present them with spirits, They regard them as not fit to be called liquor. If we give them long girdle pendants with their stones, They do not think them long enough.

There is the Milky Way in heaven [2], Which looks down on us in light; And the three stars together are the Weaving Sisters[3], Passing in a day through seven stages (of the sky).

Although they go through their seven stages, They complete no bright work for us. Brilliant Shine the Draught Oxen [4], But they do not serve to draw our carts. In the east there is Lucifer [5]; In the west there is Hesperus [6]; Long and curved

1. This stanza describes, directly or by symbol, the exactions from which the people of the east were suffering.
2. The Milky Way' is here called simply the Han, = in the sky what the Han river is in China.
3. 'The Weaving Sisters, or Ladies,' are three stars in Lyra, that form a triangle. To explain what is said of their passing through seven spaces, it is said: 'The stars seem to go round the circumference of the heavens, divided into twelve spaces, in a day and night. They would accomplish six of them in a day; but as their motion is rather in advance of that of the sun, they have entered into the seventh space by the time it is up with them again.'
4. 'The Draught Oxen' is the name of some stars in the neck of Aquila.
5. Liû Î (Sung dynasty) says: 'The metal star (Venus) is in the east in the morning, thus "opening the brightness of the day;" and it is in the west in the evening, thus "prolonging the day."' The author of the piece, however, evidently took Lucifer and Hesperus to be two stars.

is the Rabbit Net of the sky [1];—But they only occupy their places.

In the south is the Sieve [2], But it is of no use to sift. In the north is the Ladle [3], But it lades out no liquor. In the south is the Sieve, Idly showing its mouth. In the north is the Ladle, Raising its handle in the west.

The Sixth Decade, or that of Pei Shan.

ODE 3, STANZAS 1, 4, AND 5. THE HSIÂO MING.

AN OFFICER, KEPT LONG ABROAD ON DISTANT SERVICE, APPEALS TO HEAVEN, DEPLORING THE HARDSHIPS OF HIS LOT, AND TENDERS GOOD

ADVICE TO HIS MORE FORTUNATE FRIENDS AT COURT.

O bright and high Heaven, Who enlightenest and rulest this lower world! I marched on this expedition to the west, As far as this wilderness of Khiû. From the first day of the second month, I have passed through the cold and the heat. My heart is sad; The poison (of my lot) is too bitter. I think of those (at court) in their offices, And my tears flow down like rain. Do I not wish to return? But I fear the net for crime.

Ah! ye gentlemen, Do not reckon on your rest

1. 'The Rabbit Net' is the Hyades.
2. 'The Sieve' is the name of one of the twenty-eight constellations of the zodiac,—part of Sagittarius.
3. 'The Ladle' is the constellation next to 'the Sieve,'-also part of Sagittarius.

being permanent. Quietly fulfil the duties of your offices, Associating with the correct and upright; So shall the spirits hearken to you, And give you good.

Ah! ye gentlemen, Do not reckon on your repose being permanent. Quietly fulfil the duties of your offices, Loving the correct and upright; So shall the spirits hearken to you, And give you large measures of bright happiness.

ODE 5. THE KHÛ ZHZE.

SACRIFICIAL AND FESTAL SERVICES IN THE ANCESTRAL TEMPLE; AND THEIR CONNEXION WITH ATTENTION TO HUSBANDRY.

See the remarks on the Services of the Ancestral Temple, Pp. 300, 301.

Thick grew the tribulus (on the ground), But they cleared away its thorny bushes. Why did they this of old? That we might plant our millet and sacrificial millet; That our millet might be abundant, And our sacrificial millet luxuriant. When our barns are full, And our stacks can be counted by tens of myriads, We proceed to make spirits and prepared grain, For offerings and sacrifice. We seat the representatives of the dead, and urge them to eat ':-Thus seeking to increase our bright happiness.

1. The poet hurries on to describe the sacrifices in progress. The persons selected to personate the departed were necessarily inferior in rank to the principal sacrificer, yet for the time they were superior to him. This circumstance, it was supposed, would make them feel uncomfortable; and therefore, as soon as they appeared in the temple, the director of the ceremonies instructed the sacrificer to ask them to be seated, and to place them at ease; after which they were urged to take some refreshment.

With correct and reverent deportment, The bulls and rams all pure, We proceed to the winter and autumnal sacrifices. Some flay (the victims); some cook (their flesh); Some arrange (the meat); some adjust (the pieces of it). The officer of prayer sacrifices inside the temple gate[1], And all the sacrificial service is complete and brilliant. Grandly come our progenitors; Their spirits happily enjoy the offerings; Their filial descendant receives blessing:—They will reward him with great happiness, With myriads of years, life without end.

They attend to the furnaces with reverence; They prepare the trays, which are very large; Some for the roast meat, some for the broiled. Wives presiding are still and reverent 1, Preparing the numerous (smaller) dishes. The guests and visitors[3] Present the cup all round[4]. Every form is according to rule; Every smile and word are as they should be. The spirits quietly come, And respond

1. The Kû, who is mentioned here, was evidently an officer, 'one who makes or recites prayers.' The sacrifice he is said to offer was, probably, a libation, the pouring out fragrant spirits, as a part of the general service, and likely to attract the hovering spirits of the departed, on their approach to the temple. Hence his act was performed just inside the gate.
2 'Wives presiding,' i.e. the wife of the sacrificer, the principal in the service, and other ladies of the harem. The dishes under their care, the smaller dishes, would be those containing sauces, cakes, condiments, &c.
3 'The guests and visitors' would be nobles and officers of different surnames from the sacrificer, chosen by divination to take part in the sacrificial service.
4 'Present the cup all round' describes the ceremonies of drinking, which took place between the guests and visitors, the representatives of the dead, and the sacrificer.

with great blessings,—Myriads of years as the (fitting) reward.

We are very much exhausted, And have performed every ceremony without error. The able officer of prayer announces (the will of the spirits)[1]. And goes to the filial descendant to convey it[1]:—Fragrant has been your filial sacrifice, And the spirits have enjoyed your spirits and viands. They confer on you a hundred blessings; Each as it is desired, Each as sure as law. You have been exact and expeditious; You have been correct and careful; They will ever confer on you the choicest favours, In myriads and tens of myriads.'

The ceremonies having thus been completed, And the bells and drums having given their warning[2], The filial descendant goes to his place[3], And the able officer of prayer makes his announcement, 'The spirits have drunk to the full.' The great representatives of the dead then rise, And the bells and drums escort their withdrawal, (On which) the spirits tranquilly return (to whence they came)[4]. All the servants, and the presiding wives, Remove (the trays and dishes) without delay. The

1. The officer of prayer had in the first place obtained, or professed to have obtained, this answer of the progenitors from their personators.
2. The music now announced that the sacrificial service in the temple was ended.
3. The sacrificer, or principal in the service, now left the place which he had occupied, descended from the hall, and took his position at the foot of the steps on the east,—the place appropriate to him in dismissing his guests.
4. Where did they return to? According to Kâng Hsüan, 'To heaven.'

(sacrificer's) uncles and cousins All repair to the private feast[1].

The musicians all go in to perform, And give their soothing aid at the second blessing[2]. Your [3] viands are set forth; There is no dissatisfaction, but all feel happy. They drink to the full, and eat to the full; Great and small, they bow their heads., (saying), 'The spirits enjoyed your spirits and viands, And will cause you to live long. Your sacrifices, all in their seasons, Are completely discharged by you. May your sons and your grandsons Never fail to perpetuate these services!'

ODE 6. THE HSIN NAN SHAN.

HUSBANDRY TRACED TO ITS FIRST AUTHOR; DETAILS ABOUT IT, GOING ON TO THE SUBJECT OF SACRIFICES TO ANCESTORS.

The Preface refers this piece to the reign of king Yû; but there is nothing. in it to suggest the idea of its having been made in a time of disorder and misgovernment. 'The distant descendant' in the first stanza is evidently the principal in the sacrifice of the last two stanzas:—according to Kû, a noble or great landholder in the royal domain; according to others, some one of the kings of Kâu. I incline myself to this latter view. The three pieces,

1. These uncles and cousins were all present at the sacrifice, and of the same surname as the principal. The feast to them was to show his peculiar affection for his relatives.
2. The feast was given in the apartment of the temple behind the hall where the sacrifice had been performed, so that the musicians are represented as going in to continue at the feast the music they had discoursed at the sacrifice.
3. The transition to the second person here is a difficulty. We can hardly make the speech, made by some one of the guests on behalf of all the others, commence here. We must come to the conclusion that the ode was written, in compliment to the sacrificer, by one of the relatives who shared in the feast; and so here he addresses him directly.

of which this is the middle one, seem all to be royal odes. The mention of 'the southern hill' strongly confirms this view.

Yes, (all about) that southern hill Was made manageable by Yü [1]. Its plains and marshes being opened up, It was made into fields by the distant descendant. We define their boundaries, We form their smaller divisions, And make the acres lie, here to the south, there to the east.

The heavens overhead are one arch of clouds, Snowing in multitudinous flakes; There is super-added the drizzling rain. When (the land) has received the moistening, Soaking influence abundantly, It produces all our kinds of grain.

The boundaries and smaller divisions are nicely adjusted, And the millets yield abundant crops, The harvest of the distant descendant. We proceed to make therewith spirits and food, To supply our representatives of the departed, and our guests;—To obtain long life, extending over myriads of years.

In the midst of the fields are the huts[2], And

1. There is here a recognition of the work of the great Yü, as the real founder of the kingdom of China, extending the territory of former elective chiefs, and opening up the country. 'The southern hill' bounded the prospect to the south from the capital of Kâu, and hence the writer makes mention of it. He does not mean to confine the work of Yü to that part of the country; but, on the other hand, there is nothing in his language to afford a confirmation to the account given in the third Part of the SU of that hero's achievements.
2. In every King, or space of 900 Chinese acres or mâu, assigned to eight families, there were in the Centre 100 mâu of 'public fields,' belonging to the government, and cultivated by the husbandmen in common. In this space of 100 mâu, two mâu and a half were again -assigned to each family, and on them were erected the huts in which they lived, while they were actively engaged in their agricultural labours.

along the bounding divisions are gourds. The fruit is sliced and pickled, To be presented to our great ancestors, That their distant descendant may have long life, And receive the blessing of Heaven [1].

We sacrifice (first) with clear spirits, And then follow with a red bull; Offering them to our ancestors, (Our lord) holds the knife with tinkling bells, To lay open the hair of the victim, And takes the blood and fat [2].

Then we present, then we offer; All round the fragrance is diffused. Complete and brilliant is the sacrificial service; Grandly come our ancestors. They will reward (their descendant) with great blessing, Long life, years without end.

ODE 7. THE PHÛ THIEN.

PICTURES OF HUSBANDRY, AND SACRIFICES CONNECTED WITH IT. HAPPY UNDERSTANDING BETWEEN THE PEOPLE AND THEIR SUPERIORS.

It is difficult to say who the 'I' in the piece is, but evidently he and the 'distant descendant' are different persons. I suppose he may have been an officer, who had charge of the farms, as we may call them, in the royal domain.

Bright are those extensive fields, A tenth of whose produce is annually levied ³. I take the old

1. Here, as in so many other places, the sovereign Power, ruling in the lots of men, is referred to as Heaven.
2. The fat was taken from the victim, and then burnt along with fragrant herbs, so as to form a cloud of incense. On the taking of the 'blood,' it is only said, that it was done to enable the sacrificer to announce that a proper victim had been slain.
3. This line, literally, is, 'Yearly are taken ten (and a) thousand meaning the produce of ten acres in every hundred, and of a thousand in every ten thousand.

stores, And with them feed the husbandmen. From of old we have had good years; And now I go to the south-lying acres, Where some are weeding, and some gather the earth about the roots. The millets look luxuriant; And in a spacious resting place, I collect and encourage the men of greater promise ¹.

With my vessels full of bright millet, And my pure victim-rams, we sacrificed at the altar of the spirits of the land, and at (the altars of those of the four) quarters ². That my fields are in such good condition is matter of joy to the husbandmen. With lutes, and with drums beating, We will invoke the Father of Husbandry³ And pray for sweet rain, To increase the produce of our millets, And to bless my men and their wives.

The distant descendant comes, When their wives and children Are bringing food to those (at work) in the south-lying acres. The surveyor of the fields (also) comes and is glad. He takes (of the food) on the left and the right, And tastes whether

1. The general rule was that the sons of husbandmen should continue husbandmen; but their superior might select those among them in whom he saw promising abilities, and facilitate their advancement to the higher grade of officers.
2. The sacrifices here mentioned were of thanksgiving at the end of the harvest of the preceding year. The one was to 'sovereign Earth,' supposed to be the supreme Power in correlation with Heaven, or, possibly, to the spirits supposed to preside over the productive energies of the land; the other to the spirits presiding over the four quarters of the sky, and ruling all atmospherical influences.
3. This was the sacrifice that had been, or was about to be, offered in spring to 'the Father of Husbandry,'—probably the ancient mythical Tî, Shan Nang.

it be good or not. The grain is well cultivated, all, the acres over; Good will it be and abundant. The distant descendant has no displacency; The husbandmen are encouraged to diligence.

The crops of the distant descendant Look (thick) as thatch, and (swelling) like a carriage-cover. His stacks will stand like islands and mounds. He will seek for thousands of granaries; He will seek for tens of thousands of carts. The millets, the paddy, and the maize Will awake the joy of the husbandmen; (And they will say),'May he be rewarded with great happiness, With myriads of years, life without end!'

ODE 8. THE TÂ THIEN.

FURTHER PICTURES OF HUSBANDRY, AND SACRIFICES CONNECTED WITH IT.

Large are the fields, and various is the work to be done. Having selected the seed, and looked after the implements, So that all preparations have been made for our labour, We take our sharp ploughshares, And commence on the south-lying acres. We sow all the kinds of grain, Which grow up straight and large, So that the wish of the distant descendant is satisfied.

It ears and the fruit lies soft in its sheath; It hardens and is of good quality; There is no wolf's-tail grass nor darnel. We remove the insects that eat the heart and the leaf, And those that eat the roots and the joints, So that they shall not hurt the young plants of our fields. May the spirit, the Father of Husbandry[1], Lay hold of them, and put them in the blazing fire!

1. The ancient Shan Nang, as in the preceding ode.

The clouds form in dense masses,. And the rain comes down slowly. May it first rain on our public fields[1], And then come to our private Yonder shall be young grain unreaped, And here some bundles ungathered; Yonder shall be handfuls left on the ground, And here ears untouched:—For the benefit of the widow[2].

The distant descendant will come, When their wives and children Are bringing food to those (at work) on the south-lying acres. The surveyor of the fields (also) will come and be glad. They will come and offer pure sacrifices to (the spirits of the four) quarters, With their victims red and black[3], With their preparations of millet:—Thus offering, thus sacrificing, Thus increasing our bright happiness.

The Seventh Decade, or that of Sang Hû.

ODE 1, STANZA 1. THE SANG HÛ.

THE KING, ENTERTAINING THE CHIEF AMONG THE FEUDAL PRINCES, EXPRESSES HIS ADMIRATION OF THEM, AND GOOD WISHES FOR THEM.

They flit about, the greenbeaks[4], With their

1. These are two famous lines, continually quoted as showing the loyal attachment of the people to their superiors in those ancient times.
2. Compare the legislation of Moses, in connexion with the harvest, for the benefit of the poor, in Deuteronomy xxiv. 19-22.
3. They would not sacrifice to these spirits all at once, or all in one place, but in the several quarters as they went along on their progress through the domain. For each quarter the colour of the victim was different. A red victim was offered to the spirit of the south, and a black to that of the north.
4. The greenbeaks appeared in the second ode of the fifth decade. The bird had many names, and a beautiful plumage, made use of here to compliment the princes on the elegance of their manners, and perhaps also the splendour of their equipages. The bird is here called the 'mulberry Hû,' because it appeared when the mulberry tree was coming into leaf.

variegated wings, To be rejoiced in are these princes! May they receive the blessing of Heaven[1]!

ODE 6, STANZAS 1 AND 2. THE PIN KIH KHÛ YEN.

AGAINST DRUNKENNESS. DRINKING ACCORDING TO RULE AT ARCHERY CONTESTS AND THE SEASONAL SACRIFICES, AND DRINKING- TO EXCESS.

There are good grounds for referring the authorship of this piece to duke Wû of Wei (B.C. 812 to 7 58), who played an important part in the kingdom, during the affairs which terminated in the death of king Yû, and the removal of the capital from Hâo to Lo. The piece, we may suppose, is descriptive of things as they were at the court of king Yû.

When the guests first approach the mats [2], They take their, places on the left and the right in an orderly manner. The dishes of bamboo and wood are arranged in rows, With the sauces and kernels displayed in them. The spirits are mild and good, And they drink, all equally reverent. The bells and drums are properly arranged[3], And they raise their pledge-cups with order and ease [4]. (Then) the great

1. This line is to be understood, with Kû Hsî, as a prayer of the king to Heaven for his lords.
2. The mats were spread on the floor, and also the viands of the feast. Chairs and tables were not used in that early time.
3. The archery took place in the open court, beneath the hall or raised apartment, where the entertainment was given. Near the steps leading up to the hall was the regular place for the bells and drums, but it was necessary now to remove them more on one side, to leave the ground clear for the archers.
4. The host first presented a cup to the guest, which the latter drank, and then be returned a cup to the host. After this preliminary ceremony, the company all drank to one another,—'took up their cups,' as it is here expressed.

target is set up; The bows and arrows are made ready for the shooting. The archers are arranged in classes; 'Show your skill in shooting,' (it is said by one). 'I shall hit that mark' (is the response), 'And pray you to drink the cup[1]'.

The dancers move with their flutes to the notes of the organ and drum, While all the instruments perform in harmony. All this is done to please the meritorious ancestors, Along with the observance of all ceremonies. When all the ceremonies have been fully performed, Grandly and fully, (The personators of the dead say), 'We confer on you great blessings, And may your descendants, also be happy!' These are happy and delighted, And each of them exerts his ability. A guest [2] draws the spirits; An attendant enters again with a cup, And fills it,—the cup of rest [2]. Thus are performed your seasonal ceremonies[3].

1. Each defeated archer was obliged to drink a large cup of spirits as a penalty
2. This guest was, it is supposed, the eldest of all the scions of the royal House present on the occasion. At this point, he presented a cup to the chief among the personators of the ancestors, and received one in return. He then proceeded to draw more spirits from one of the vases of supply, and an attendant came in

and filled other cups,—we may suppose for all the other personators. This was called 'the cup of repose or comfort;' and the sacrifice was thus concluded,—in all sobriety and decency.

3. The three stanzas that follow this, graphically descriptive of the drunken revel, are said to belong to the feast of the royal relatives that followed the conclusion of the sacrificial service, and is called 'the second blessing' in the sixth ode of the preceding decade. This opinion probably is correct; but as the piece does not itself say so, and because of the absence from the text of religious sentiments, I have not given the stanzas here.

The Eighth Decade, or that of Po Hwâ.

ODE 5, STANZAS 1 AND 2. THE PO HWÂ.

THE QUEEN OF KING YÛ COMPLAINS OF BEING DEGRADED AND FORSAKEN.

The fibres from the white-flowered rush Are bound with the white grass[1]. This man's sending me away makes me dwell solitary.

The light and brilliant clouds Bedew the rush and the grass[2]. The way of Heaven is hard and difficult[3];—This man does not conform (to good principle).

1. The stalks of the rush were tied with the grass in bundles, in order to be steeped;- an operation which ladies in those days might be supposed to be familiar with. The two lines suggest the idea of the close connexion between the two plants, and the necessariness of the one to the other;-as it should be between husband and wife.
2. The clouds bestowed their dewy influence on the plants, while her husband neglected the speaker.
3. The way of Heaven' is equivalent to our 'The course of Providence.' The lady's words are, literally, 'The steps of Heaven.' She makes but a feeble wail; but in Chinese opinion discharges thereby, all the better, the duty of a wife.

III.

THE MAJOR ODES OF THE KINGDOM.

PIECES AND STANZAS ILLUSTRATING THE RELIGIOUS VIEWS AND PRACTICES OF THE WRITERS AND THEIR TIMES.

The First Decade, or that of Wan Wang.

ODE 1. THE WAN WANG.

CELEBRATING KING WAN, DEAD AND ALIVE, AS THE FOUNDER OF THE DYNASTY OF KÂU, SHOWING HOW HIS VIRTUES DREW TO HIM THE FAVOURING REGARD Or HEAVEN OR GOD, AND MADE HIM A BRIGHT PATTERN TO HIS DESCENDANTS AND THEIR MINISTERS

The composition of this and the other pieces of this decade is attributed to the duke of Kâu, king Wan's son, and was intended by him for the benefit of his nephew, the young king Khang. Wan, it must be borne in mind, was never actually king of China. He laid the foundations of the kingly power, which was established by his son king Wû, and consolidated by the duke of Kâu. The title of king was given to him and to others by the duke, according to the view of filial piety, that has been referred to on p. 299.

King Wan is on high. Oh! bright is he in heaven. Although Kâu was an old country, The (favouring) appointment lighted on it recently'. Illustrious was the House of Kâu, And the

1. The family of Kâu, according to its traditions, was very ancient, but it did not occupy the territory of Kâu, from which it subsequently took its name, till B.C. 1326; and it was not till the time of Wan (B.C. 1231 to 1135) that the divine purpose concerning its supremacy in the kingdom was fully manifested.

appointment of God came at the proper season. King Wan ascends and descends On the left and the right of God[1].

Full of earnest activity was king Wan, And his fame is without end. The gifts (of God) to Kâu Extend to the descendants of king Wan, In the direct line and the collateral branches for a hundred generations[2]. All the officers of Kâu Shall (also) be illustrious from age to age.

They shall be illustrious from age to age, Zealously and reverently pursuing their plans. Admirable are the many officers, Born in this royal kingdom. The royal kingdom is able to produce them, The supporters of (the House of) Kâu. Numerous is the array of officers, And by them king Wan enjoys his repose.

Profound was king Wan; Oh! continuous and bright was his feeling of reverence. Great is the appointment of Heaven! There were the descendants of (the sovereigns of) Shang,-The descendants of the sovereigns of Shang Were in number more

1. According to Kû Hsî, the first and last two lines of this stanza are to be taken of the spirit of Wan in heaven. Attempts have been made to explain them otherwise, or rather to explain them away. But language could not more expressly intimate the existence of a supreme personal God, and the continued existence of the human spirit.
2. The text, literally, is, 'The root and the branches:' the root (and stem) denoting the eldest sons, by the recognised queen, succeeding to the throne; and the branches, the other sons by the queen and concubines. The former would grow up directly from the root; and the latter, the chief nobles of the kingdom, would constitute the branches of the great Kâu tree.
3. The Shang or Yin dynasty of kings superseded by Kâu.

than hundreds of thousands. But when God gave the command, They became subject to Kâu.

They became subject to Kâu, (For) the appointment of Heaven is not unchangeable. The officers of Yin, admirable and alert,

Assist at the libations in our capital[1]. They assist at those libations, Always wearing the hatchet-figures on their lower garments and their peculiar cap[2]. O ye loyal ministers of the king, Ever think of your ancestor!

Ever think of your ancestor, Cultivating your virtue, Always seeking to accord with the will (of Heaven):-So shall you be seeking for much happiness, Before Yin lost the multitudes, (Its kings) were the correlates of God'. Look to Yin as a beacon i The great appointment is not easily preserved.

The appointment is not easily (preserved):—Do not cause your own extinction. Display and make bright your righteousness and fame, And look at (the fate of) Yin in the light of Heaven. The doings of high Heaven Have neither sound nor

1. These officers of Yin would be the descendants of the Yin kings and of their principal nobles, scions likewise of the, Yin stock. They would assist, at the court of Kâu, at the services in the ancestral temple, which began with a libation of fragrant spirits to bring down the spirits of the departed.
2. These, differing from the dress worn by the representatives of the ruling House, were still worn by the officers of Yin or Shang, by way of honour, and also by way of warning.
3. There was God in heaven hating none, desiring the good of all the people; there were the sovereigns on earth, God's vicegerents, maintained by him so long as they carried out in their government his purpose of good.

smell[1]. Take your pattern from king Wan, And the myriad regions will repose confidence in you.

ODE 2. THE TÂ MING.

HOW THE APPOINTMENT OF HEAVEN OR GOD CAME FROM HIS FATHER TO KING WAN, AND DESCENDED TO HIS SON, KING WÛ, WHO OVERTHREW THE DYNASTY OF SHANG BY HIS VICTORY AT MÛ, CELEBRATING ALSO THE MOTHER AND WIFE OF KING WAN.

The illustration of illustrious (virtue) is required below, And the dread majesty is or, high[2]. Heaven is not readily to be relied on;

It is not easy to be king. Yin's rightful heir to the heavenly seat Was not permitted to possess the kingdom.

Zan, the second of the princesses of Kih[3], From (the domain of) Yin-shang, Came to be married to (the prince of) Kâu, And became his wife in his

1. These two lines are quoted in the last paragraph of the Doctrine of the Mean, as representing the ideal of perfect virtue. They are indicative of Power, operating silently, and not to be perceived by the senses, but resistless in its operations.
2. 'The first two lines,' says the commentator Yen Zhan, 'contain a general sentiment, expressing the principle that governs the relation between Heaven and men. According to line 1, the good or evil of a ruler cannot be-concealed; according to 2, Heaven, in giving its favour or taking it away, acts with strict decision. When below there is the illustrious illustration (of virtue), that reaches up on high. When above there is the awful majesty, that exercises a survey below. The relation between Heaven and men ought to excite our awe.'
3. The state of Kih must have been somewhere in the royal domain of Yin. Its lords had the surname of Zan, and the second daughter of the House became the wife of Kî of Kâu. She is called in the eighth line Thâi-zan, by which name she is still famous in China. 'She commenced,' it is said, 'the instruction of her child when he was still in her womb, looking on no improper sight, listening to no licentious sound, uttering no word of pride.'

capital. Both she and king Kî Were entirely virtuous. (Then) Thâi-zan became pregnant, And gave birth to our king Wan.

This king Wan, Watchfully and reverently, With entire intelligence served God, And so secured the great blessing. His virtue was without deflection; And in consequence he received (the allegiance of) the states from all quarters.

Heaven surveyed this lower world; And its appointment lighted (on king Wan). In his early years, It made for him a mate[1];— On the north of the Hsiâ, On the banks of the Wei. When king Wan would marry, There was the lady in a large state[2].

In a large state was the lady, Like a fair denizen of heaven. The ceremonies determined the auspiciousness (of the union)[3], And in person he met her on the Wei. Over it he made a bridge of boats; The glory (of the occasion) was illustrious.

The favouring appointment was from Heaven, Giving the throne to our kin Wan, In the capital of Kâu. The lady-successor was from Hsin, Its eldest daughter, who came to marry him. She was blessed to give birth to king Wû, Who was preserved, and helped, and received (also) the. appointment,

1. Heaven is here represented as arranging for the fulfilment of its purposes beforehand.
2. The name of the state was Hsin, and it must have been near the Hsiâ and the Wei, somewhere in the south-east of the present Shen-hsî.
3. 'The ceremonies' would be various; first of all, divination by means of the tortoise-shell.

And in accordance with it smote the great Shang.

The troops of Yin-shang Were collected like a forest, And marshalled in the wilderness of Mû. We rose (to the crisis); 'God is with you,' (said Shang-fû to the king), 'Have no doubts in your heart[1].'

The wilderness of Mû spread out extensive; Bright shone the chariots of sandal; The teams of bays, black-maned and white-bellied, galloped along; The Grand-Master Shang-fû. Was like an eagle on the wing, Assisting king Wû, Who at one onset smote the great Shang. That morning's encounter was followed by a clear, bright (day).

ODE 3. THE MIEN.

SMALL BEGINNINGS AND SUBSEQUENT GROWTH OF THE HOUSE OF KÂU IN KÂU. ITS REMOVAL FROM PIN UNDER THAN-FÛ, WITH ITS FIRST SETTLEMENT IN KÂU, WITH THE PLACE THEN GIVEN TO THE BUILDING OF THE ANCESTRAL TEMPLE, AND THE ALTAR TO THE SPIRITS OF THE LAND. CONSOLIDATION OF ITS FORTUNES BY KING WAN.

'The ancient duke Than-fû' was the grandfather of king Wan, and was canonized by the duke of Kâu as 'king Thâi.' As mentioned in a note on p. 316, he was the first of his family to settle in Kâu, removing there from Pin, the site of their earlier settlement, 'the country about the Khü and the Khî.'

In long trains ever increasing grow the gourds[2]. When (our) people first sprang, From the country about the Khü and the Khî[1], The ancient duke

1. See the account of the battle of Mû in the third Book of the fifth Part of the Shû. Shang-fû was one of Wû's principal leaders and counsellors, his 'Grand-Master Shang-fû' in the next stanza.
2. As a gourd grows and extends, with a vast development of its tendrils and leaves, so had the House of Kâu increased.
3. These were two rivers in the territory of Pin, which name still remains in the small department of Pin Kâu, in Shen-hsî. The Khü flows into the Lo, and the Khî into the Wei.

Than-fû Made for them kiln-like huts and caves, Ere they had yet any houses [1].

The ancient duke Than-fû Came in the morning, galloping his horses, Along the banks of the western rivers, To the foot of mount Khî[2]; And there he and the lady Kiang[3] Came and together looked out for a site.

The plain of Kâu looked beautiful and rich, With its violets, and sowthistles (sweet) as dumplings. There he began by consulting (with his followers); There he singed the tortoise-shell, (and divined). The responses were there to stay and then; And they proceeded there to build[4].

He encouraged the people, and settled them; Here on the left, there on the right. He divided the ground, and subdivided it; If he dug the ditches; he defined the acres. From the east to the west, There was nothing which he did not take in hand [5].

1. According to this ode then, up to the time of Than-fû, the Kâu people had only had the dwellings here described; but this is not easily reconciled with other accounts, or even with other stanzas of this piece.
2. See a graphic account of the circumstances in which this migration took place, in the fifteenth chapter of the second Part of the first Book of Mencius, very much to the honour of the ancient duke.
3. This lady is known as Thâi-kiang, the worthy predecessor of Thâi-zan.
4. This stanza has reference to the choice—by council and divination—of a site for what should be the chief town of the new settlement.
5. This stanza describes the general arrangements for the occupancy and cultivation of the plain of Kâu, and the distribution of the people over it.

He called his Superintendent of Works; He called his Minister of Instruction; And charged them with the rearing of the houses. With the line they made everything straight; They bound the frame-boards tight, so that they should rise regularly uprose the ancestral temple in its solemn grandeur[1].

Crowds brought the earth in baskets; They threw it with shouts into the frames; They beat it with responsive blows. They pared the walls repeatedly, till they sounded strong. Five thousand cubits of them arose together, So that the roll of the great drums did not overpower (the noise of the builders)[2].

They reared the outer gate (of the palace), Which rose in lofty state. They set up the gate of audience, Which rose severe and exact. They reared the great altar to the spirits of the land, From which all great movements should proceed[3].

1. This stanza describes the preparations and processes for erecting the buildings of the new city. The whole took place under the direction of two officers, in whom we have the germ probably of the Six Heads of the Boards or Departments, whose functions are described in the Shû and the Official Book of Kâu. The materials of the buildings were earth and lime pounded together in frames, as is still to be seen in many parts of the country. The first great building taken in hand was the ancestral temple. Than-fit would make a home for the spirits of his fathers, before he made one for himself. However imperfectly directed, the religious feeling asserted the supremacy which it ought to possess.
2. The bustle and order of the building all over the city is here graphically set forth.
3. Than-fû was now at leisure to build the palace for himself, which appears to have been not a very large building, though the Chinese names of its gates are those belonging to the two which were peculiar to the palaces of the kings of Kâu in the subsequent times of the dynasty. Outside the palace were the altars appropriate to the spirits of the four quarters of the land, the 'great' or royal altar being peculiar to the kings, though the one built by Than-fû is here so named. All great undertakings, and such as required the co-operation of all the people, were preceded by a solemn sacrifice at this altar.

Thus though he could not prevent the rage of his foes[1], He did not let fall his own fame. The oaks and the buckthorns were (gradually) thinned, And roads for travellers were opened. The hordes of the Khwan disappeared, Startled and panting.

(The chiefs of) Yü and Zui [2] were brought to an agreement By king Wan's stimulating their natural virtue. Then, I may say, some came to him, previously not knowing him; Some, drawn the last by the first; Some, drawn by his rapid successes, And some by his defence (of the weak) from insult.

1. Referring to Than-fû's relations with the wild hordes, described by Mencius, and which obliged him to leave Pin. As the new settlement in Kâu grew, they did not dare to trouble it.
2. The poet passes on here to the time of king Wan. The story of the chiefs of Yü and Zui (two states on the east of the Ho) is this:—They had a quarrel about a strip of

territory, to which each of them laid claim. Going to lay their dispute before the lord of Kâu, as soon as they entered his territory, they saw the ploughers readily yielding the furrow, and travellers yielding the path, while men and women avoided one another on the road, and old people had no burdens to carry. At his court, they beheld the officers of each inferior grade giving place to those above them. They became ashamed of their own quarrel, agreed to let the disputed ground be an open territory, and withdrew without presuming to appear, before Wan. When this affair was noised abroad, more than forty states, it is said, tendered their submission to Kâu.

ODE 4, STANZAS 1 AND 2. THE YÎ PHO.

IN PRAISE OF KING WAN, CELEBRATING HIS INFLUENCE, DIGNITY IN THE TEMPLE SERVICES, ACTIVITY, AND CAPACITY TO RULE.

Abundant is the growth of the buckthorn and shrubby trees, Supplying firewood; yea, stores of it[1]. Elegant and dignified was our prince and king; On the left and the right they hastened to him.

Elegant and dignified was our prince and king; On his left and his right they bore their half-mace (libation-cups)[2]:—They bore them with solemn gravity, As beseemed such eminent officers.

ODE 5. THE HAN LÛ.

IN PRAISE OF THE VIRTUE OF KING WAN, BLESSED BY HIS ANCESTORS, AND RAISED TO THE HIGHEST DIGNITY WITHOUT' SEEKING OF HIS OWN.

Look at the foot of the Han[3], How abundantly grow the hazel and arrow-thorn[4]. Easy and self-possessed was our prince, In his pursuit of dignity (still) easy and self-possessed.

Massive is that libation-cup of jade, With the

1. It is difficult to trace the connexion between-these allusive lines and the rest of the piece.
2. Here we have the lord of Kâu in his ancestral temple, assisted by his ministers or great officers in pouring out the libations to the spirits of the departed. The libation-cup was fitted with a handle of jade, that used by the king having a complete kwei, the obelisk-like symbol of rank, while the cups used by a minister had for a handle only half a kwei.

3. Where mount Han was cannot now be determined.
4. As the foot of the hill was favourable to vegetable growth, so were king Wan's natural qualities to his distinction and advancement.

yellow liquid sparkling in it[1]. Easy and self-possessed was our prince, The fit recipient of blessing and dignity.

The hawk flies up to heaven, The fishes leap in the deep [2]. Easy and self-possessed was our prince:—Did he not exert an influence on men?

His clear spirits were in the vessels; His red bull was ready[3];— To offer, to sacrifice, To increase his bright happiness.

Thick grow the oaks and the buckthorn, Which the people use for fuel [4]. Easy and self-possessed was our prince, Cheered and encouraged by the spirits [4].

Luxuriant are the dolichos and other creepers, Clinging to the branches and stems. Easy and self-possessed was our prince, Seeking for happiness by no crooked ways.

ODE 6. THE SZE KÂI.

THE VIRTUE OF WAN, WITH HIS FILIAL PIETY AND CONSTANT REVERENCE, AND THEIR WONDERFUL EFFECTS. THE EXCELLENT CHARACTER OF HIS MOTHER AND WIFE.

Pure and reverent was Thâi Zan[5], The mother of king Wan. Loving was she to Kâu Kiang [6];—

1. As a cup of such quality was the proper receptacle for the yellow, herb-flavoured spirits, so was the character of Wan such that all blessing must accrue to him.
2. It is the nature of the hawk to fly and of fishes to swim, and so there went out an influence from Wan unconsciously to himself.
3. Red, we have seen, was the proper colour for victims in the ancestral temple of Kâu.
4. As it was natural for the people to take the wood and use it, so it was natural for the spirits of his ancestors, and spiritual beings generally, to bless king Wan.
5. Thâi Zan is celebrated, above, in the second ode.
6. Kâu Kiang is 'the lady Kiang' of ode 3, the wife of Than-fû or king Thâi, who came with him from Pin. She is here called Kâu, as having married the lord of Kâu.

A wife becoming the House of Kâu. Thâi Sze [1] inherited her excellent fame, And from her came a hundred sons [2].

He conformed to the example of his ancestors, And their spirits had no occasion for complaint. Their spirits had no occasion for dissatisfaction; And his example acted on his wife, Extended to his brethren, And was felt by all the clans and states.

Full of harmony was he in his palace; Full of reverence in the ancestral temple. Unseen (by men), he still felt that he was under inspection[3]: Unweariedly he maintained his virtue.

Though he could not prevent (some) great calamities, His brightness and magnanimity were without stain. Without previous instruction he did what was right; Without admonition he went on (in the path of goodness).

So, grown. up men became virtuous (through him), And young men made (constant) attainments. (Our) ancient prince never felt weariness, And from him were the fame and eminence of his officers.

1. Thâi Sze, the wife of Wan, we are told in ode 2, was from the state of Hsin. The surname Sze shows that its lords must have been descended from the Great Yü.
2. We are not to suppose that Thâi Sze had herself a hundred sons. She had ten, and her freedom from jealousy so encouraged the fruitfulness of the harem, that all the sons born in it are ascribed to her.
3. Where there was no human eye to observe him, Wan still felt that he was open to the observation of spiritual beings.

ODE 7. THE HWANG Î.

SHOWING THE RISE OF THE HOUSE OF KÂU TO THE SOVEREIGNTY OF THE KINGDOM THROUGH THE FAVOUR OF GOD, THE ACHIEVEMENTS OF KINGS THÂI AND KÎ, AND ESPECIALLY OF KING WAN.

Great is God, Beholding this lower world in majesty. He surveyed the four quarters (of the kingdom), Seeking for some one to give establishment to the people. Those two earlier dynasties [1] Had failed to satisfy him with their government; So, throughout the various states, He sought and considered For one on whom he might confer the rule. Hating all the great states, He turned his kind regards on the west, And there gave a settlement (to king Thâi).

(King Thâi) raised up and removed The dead trunks and the fallen trees. He dressed and regulated The bushy clumps and the (tangled) rows. He opened up and cleared The tamarisk trees and the stave trees. He hewed and thinned The mountain mulberry trees. God having brought about the removal thither of this intelligent ruler, The Kwan hordes fled away[2]. Heaven had raised up a helpmeet for him, And the appointment he had received was made sure.

God surveyed the hills, Where the oaks and the buckthorn were thinned, And paths made through the firs and cypresses. God, who had raised the

1. Those of Hsiâ and Shang.
2. The same as 'the hordes of the Khwan' in ode 3. Mr. T. W. Kingsmill says that 'Kwan' here should be 'Chun,' and charges the transliteration Kwan with error (Journal of the Royal Asiatic Society for April, 1878). He had not consulted his dictionary for the proper pronunciation of the Chinese character.

state, raised up a proper ruler[1] for it,—From the time of Thâi-po and king Kî (this was done)[1]. Now this king Kî In his heart was full of brotherly duty. Full of duty to his elder brother, He gave himself the more to promote the prosperity (of the country), And secured to him the glory (of his act)[2]. He accepted his dignity and did not lose it, And (ere long his family) possessed the whole kingdom.

This king Kî Was gifted by God with the power of judgment, So that the fame of his virtue silently grew. His virtue was highly intelligent,—Highly intelligent, and of rare discrimination; Able to lead, able to rule, To rule over this great country; Rendering a cordial submission, effecting a cordial union[3]. When (the sway) came to king Wan, His

1 King Wan is 'the proper ruler' intended here, and the next line intimates that this was determined before there was any likelihood of his becoming the ruler even of the territory of Kâu; another instance of the foreseeing providence ascribed to God. Thâi-po was the eldest son of king Thai, and king Kî was, perhaps, only the third. The succession ought to have come to Thai-po; but he, seeing the sage virtues of Khang (afterwards king Wan), the son of Kî, and seeing also that king Thai was anxious that this boy should ultimately become ruler of Kâu, voluntarily withdrew from Kau altogether, and left the state to Kî and his son. See the remark of Confucius on Thâi-po's conduct, in the Analects, VIII, i.

2. The lines from six to ten speak of king Kî in his relation to his elder brother. He accepted Thâi-po's act without -any failure of his own duty to him, and by his own improvement of it, made his brother more glorious through it. His feeling of brotherly duty was simply the natural instinct of his heart. Having accepted the act, it only made him the more anxious to promote the good of the state, and thus he made his brother more glorious by showing what advantages accrued from his resignation and withdrawal from Kau.

3. This line refers to Kî's maintenance of his own loyal duty to the dynasty of Shang, and his making all the states under his presidency loyal also.

virtue left nothing to be dissatisfied with, He received the blessing of God, And it was extended to his descendants.

God said to king Wan [1], 'Be not like those who reject this and cling to that; Be not like those who are ruled by their likings and desires;' So he grandly ascended before others to the height (of virtue). The people of Mî [2] were disobedient, Daring to oppose our great country, And invaded Yüan, marching to Kung [3]. The king rose, majestic in his wrath; He marshalled his troops, To stop the invading foes; To consolidate the prosperity of Kâu; To meet the expectations of all under heaven.

He remained quietly in the capital, But (his troops) went on from the borders of Yüan. They ascended our lofty ridges, And (the enemy) arrayed no forces on our hills, On our hills, small or large, Nor drank at our springs, Our springs or our pools. He then determined the finest of the plains, And settled on the south of Khî [4], On the banks of

1. The statement that 'God spake to king Wan,' repeated in stanza 7, vexes the Chinese critics, and they find in it simply an intimation that Wan's conduct was 'in accordance with the will of Heaven.' I am not prepared to object to that view of the meaning; but it is plain that the writer, in giving such a form to his meaning, must have conceived of God as a personal Being, knowing men's hearts, and able to influence them.
2. Mî or Mî-hsü was a state in the present King-ning Kâu, of Phing-liang department, Kan-sû.
3. Yüan was a state adjacent to Mî,—the present King Kâu, and Kung must have been a place or district in it.
4 Wan, it appears, made now a small change in the site of his capital, but did not move to Fang, where he finally settled.

the Wei, The centre of all the states, The resort of the lower people.

God said to king Wei, 'I am pleased with your intelligent virtue, Not loudly proclaimed nor pourtrayed, Without extravagance or

112

changeableness, Without consciousness of effort on your part, In accordance with the pattern of God.' God said to king Wăn, 'Take measures against the country of your foes. Along with your 'brethren, Get ready your scaling ladders, And your engines of onfall and assault, To attack the walls of Khung[1].'

The engines of onfall and assault were (at first) gently plied, Against the walls of Khung high and great; Captives for the question were brought in, one after another; The left ears (of the slain) were taken leisurely 2. He had sacrificed to God and to the Father of War 3, Thus seeking to induce

1. Khung was a state, in the present district of Hû, department Hsî-an, Shen-hsî. His conquest of Khung was an important event in the history of king Wăn. He moved his capital to it, advancing so much farther towards the east, nearer to the domain of-Shang. According to Sze-mg Khien the marquis of Khung had slandered the lord of Kâu, who was president of the states of the west, to Kau-hsin, the king of Shang, and our hero was put in prison. His friends succeeded in effecting his deliverance by means of various gifts to the tyrant, and he was reinstated In the west with more than his former power. Three years afterwards he attacked the marquis of Khung.
2. So far the siege was prosecuted slowly and, so to say, tenderly, Wăn hoping that the enemy would be induced to surrender without great sacrifice of life.
3. The sacrifice to God had been offered in Kâu, at the commencement of the expedition; that to the Father of War, on the army's arriving at the borders of Khung. We can hardly tell who is intended by the Father of War. Kû Hsî and others would require the plural 'Fathers,' saying the sacrifice was to Hwang Tî and Khih Yû, who are found engaged in hostilities far back in the mythical period of Chinese history. But Khih Yû appears as a rebel, or opposed to the One man in all the country who was then fit to rule. It is difficult to imagine how they could be associated, and sacrificed to together.

submission, And throughout the region none had dared to insult him. The engines of onfall and assault were (then) vigorously plied, Against the walls of Khung very strong. He attacked it, and let loose all his forces; He extinguished (its sacrifices) [1], and made an end of its existence; And throughout the kingdom none dared to oppose him.

ODE 9. THE HSIÂ WÛ.

IN PRAISE OF KING WÛ, WALKING IN THE WAYS OF HIS FOREFATHERS, AND BY HIS FILIAL PIETY SECURING THE THRONE TO HIMSELF AND HIS POSTERITY.

Successors tread in the steps (of their predecessors) in our Kâu. For generations there had been wise kings; The three sovereigns were in heaven [2]; And king (Wû) was their worthy successor in his capital [3].

King (Wû) was their worthy successor in his capital, Rousing himself to seek for the hereditary virtue, Always striving to be in accordance with the

1. The extinction of its sacrifices was the final act in the extinction of a state. Any members of its ruling House who might survive could no longer sacrifice to their ancestors as having been men of princely dignity. The family was reduced to the ranks of the people.
2. 'The three sovereigns,' or 'wise kings,' are to be understood of the three celebrated in ode 7,—Thâi, Kî, and Wan. We are thus obliged, with all Chinese scholars, to understand this ode of king Wû. The statement that 'the three kings were in heaven' is very express.
3. The capital here is Hâo, to which Wû removed in B.C. 1134, the year after his father's death. It was on the east of the river Fang, and only about eight miles from Wan's capital of Fang.

will (of Heaven); And thus he secured the confidence due to a king.

He secured the confidence due to a king, And became the pattern of all below him. Ever thinking how to be filial, His filial mind was the model (which he supplied).

Men loved him, the One man, And responded (to his example) with a docile virtue. Ever thinking how to be filial, He brilliantly continued the doings (of his fathers).

Brilliantly! and his posterity, Continuing to walk in the steps of their forefathers, For myriads of years, Will receive the blessing of Heaven.

They will receive the blessing of Heaven, And from the four quarters (of the kingdom) will felicitations come to them. For myriads of years Will there not be their helpers?

ODE 10. THE WAN WANG YÛ SHANG.

THE PRAISE OF KINGS WAN AND WÛ:-HOW THE FORMER DISPLAYED HIS MILITARY PROWESS ONLY TO SECURE THE TRANQUILLITY OF THE PEOPLE; AND HOW THE LATTER, IN ACCORDANCE WITH THE RESULTS OF DIVINATION, ENTERED IN HIS NEW CAPITAL OF HÂO, INTO THE SOVEREIGNTY OF THE KINGDOM WITH THE SINCERE GOOD WILL OF ALL THE PEOPLE.

King Wăn is famous; Yea, he is very famous. What he sought was the repose (of the people); What he saw was the completion (of his work). A sovereign true was king Wăn!

King Wăn received the appointment (from Heaven), And achieved his martial success. Having overthrown Khung[1]. He fixed his (capital) city in Fang [2]. A sovereign true was king Wăn!

1. As related in ode 7.
2. Fang had, probably, been the capital of Khung, and Wăn removed to it, simply making the necessary repairs and alterations. This explains how we find nothing about the divinations which should have preceded so important a step as the founding of a new capital.

He repaired the walls along the (old) moat. His establishing himself in Fang was according to (the pattern of his forefathers), It was not that he was in haste to gratify his wishes;—It was to show the filial duty that had come down to him. A sovereign true was the royal prince!

His royal merit was brightly displayed By those walls of Fang. There were collected (the sympathies of the people of) the four quarters, Who regarded the royal prince as their protector. A sovereign true was the royal prince!

The Fang-water flowed on to the east (of the city), Through the meritorious labour of Yü. There were collected (the sympathies of the people of) the four quarters, Who would have the great king as their ruler. A sovereign true was the great king

In the capital of Hâo he built his hall with its circlet of water [2]. From the west to the east, From the south to the north, There was not a thought but did him homage. A sovereign true was the great king!

He examined and divined, did the king, About settling in the capital of Hâo. The tortoise-shell decided the site[3], And king Wû completed the city. A sovereign true was king Wû!

1. The writer has passed on to Wû, who did actually become king.
2. See on the third of the Praise Odes of Lû in Part IV.
3. Hâo was built by Wû, and hence we have the account of his divining About the site and the undertaking.

By the Fang-water grows the white millet[1];—Did not king Wû show wisdom in his employment of officers? He would leave his plans to his descendants, And secure comfort and support to his son. A sovereign true was king Wû!

The Second Decade, or that of Shang Min.

ODE 1. THE SHANG MIN.

THE LEGEND OF HÂU-KÎ:—HIS CONCEPTION; HIS BIRTH; THE PERILS OF HIS INFANCY; HIS BOYISH HABITS OF AGRICULTURE; HIS SUBSEQUENT METHODS AND TEACHING OF AGRICULTURE; HIS FOUNDING OF CERTAIN SACRIFICES; AND THE HONOURS OF SACRIFICE PAID TO HIM BY THE HOUSE OF KÂU.

Of Hâu-kî there is some notice on the tenth ode of the first decade of the Sacrificial Odes of Kâu. To him the kings of Kâu traced their lineage. Of Kiang Yüan, his mother, our knowledge is very scanty. It is said that she was a daughter of the House of Thâi, which traced its lineage up to Shan-nung in prehistoric times. From the first stanza of this piece it appears that she was married, and had been so for some time without having any child. But who her husband was it is impossible to say with certainty. As the Kâu surname was Kî, he must have been one of the descendants of Hwang Tî.

The first birth of (our) people[2] Was from Kiang Yüan. How did she give birth to (our) people She had presented a pure offering and sacrificed[3],

1. 'The white millet,' a valuable species, grown near the Fang, suggests to the writer the idea of all the men of ability whom Wû collected around him.
2. Our 'people' is of course the people of Kâu. The whole piece is about the individual from whom the House of Kâu sprang, of which were the kings of the dynasty so called.
3. To whom Kiang Yüan sacrificed and prayed we are not told, but I receive the impression that it was to God,—see the next stanza,—and that she did so all alone with the special object which is mentioned.

That her childlessness might be taken away. She then trod on a toe-print made by God, and was moved[1], In the large place where she rested. She became pregnant; she dwelt retired; She gave birth to, and nourished (a son), Who was Hâu-kî.

When she had fulfilled her months, Her firstborn son (came forth) like a lamb. There was no bursting, nor rending, No injury, no hurt; Showing how wonderful he would be. Did not God give her the comfort? Had he not accepted her pure offering and sacrifice, So that thus easily she brought forth her son?

He was placed in a narrow lane, But the sheep and oxen protected him with loving care[2]. He was placed in a wide forest, Where he was met with by the wood-cutters. He was placed on the cold ice, And a bird screened and supported him with its wings. When the bird went away, Hâu-kî began to wail. His cry was long and loud, So that his voice filled the whole way[2].

1. The 'toe-print made by God' has occasioned much speculation of the critics. We may simply draw the conclusion that the poet meant to have his readers believe with him that the conception of his hero was supernatural. We saw in the third of the Sacrificial Odes of Shang that there was also a legend assigning a præternatural birth to the father of the House of Shang
2. It does not appear from the ode who exposed the infant to these various perils; nor did Chinese tradition ever fashion any story on the subject. Mâo makes the exposure to have been made by Mang Yüan's husband, dissatisfied with what had taken place; Kang, by the mother herself, to show the more the wonderful character of her child. Readers will compare the accounts with the Roman legends about Romulus and Remus, their mother and her father; but the two legends differ according to the different characters, of the Chinese and Roman peoples.

When he was able to crawl, He looked majestic and intelligent. When he was able to feed himself, He fell to planting beans. The beans grew luxuriantly; His rows of paddy shot up beautifully; His hemp and wheat grew strong and close; His gourds yielded abundantly.

The husbandry of Hâu-kî Proceeded on the plan of helping (the growth). Having cleared away the thick grass, He sowed the ground with the yellow cereals. He managed the living grain, till it was ready to burst; Then he used it as seed, and it sprang up; It grew and came into ear; It became strong and good; It hung down, every grain complete; And thus he was appointed lord of Thâi[1].

He gave (his people) the beautiful grains;-The black millet and the double-kernelled, The tall red and the white. They planted extensively the black and the double-kernelled, Which were reaped and stacked on the ground. They planted extensively the tall red and the white, Which were carried on their shoulders and backs, Home for the sacrifices which he founded[1].

And how as to our sacrifices (continued from him)?

1. Hâu-kî's mother, we have seen, was a princess of Thâi, in the present district of Wû-kung, Khien Kau, Shen-hsî. This may have led to his appointment to that principality, and the transference of the lordship from Kiangs to Kîs. Evidently he was appointed to that dignity for his services in the promotion of agriculture. Still he not displaced the older Shan-nung, with whom on his father's side he had a connexion, as 'the Father of Husbandry.'
2. This is not to be understood of sacrifice in general, as if there had been no such thing before Hâu-kî; but of the sacrifices of the of House of Kâu,—those in the ancestral temple and others,—which began with him as its great ancestor.

Some hull (the grain); some take it from the mortar; Some sift it; some tread it. It is rattling in the dishes; It is distilled, and the steam floats about. We consult[1]; we observe the rites of purification; We take southernwood and offer it with the fat; We sacrifice a ram to the spirit of the path[2]; We offer roast flesh and broiled:—And thus introduce the coming year[3].

We load the stands with the offerings, The stands both of wood and of earthenware. As soon as the fragrance ascends, God, well pleased, smells the sweet savour. Fragrant it is, and in its due season[4]. Hâu-kî founded our sacrifices, And no one, we presume, has given occasion for blame or regret in regard to them, Down to the present day.

ODE 2. THE HSIN WEI.

A FESTAL ODE, CELEBRATING SOME ENTERTAINMENT GIVEN BY THE KING TO HIS RELATIVES, WITH THE TRIAL OF ARCHERY AFTER THE FEAST; CELEBRATING ESPECIALLY THE HONOUR DONE ON SUCH OCCASIONS TO THE AGED.

This ode is given here, because it is commonly taken as a prelude to the next. Kû Hsî interprets it of the feast, given by, the

1. That is, we divine about the day, and choose the officers to take part in the service.
2. A sacrifice was offered to the spirit of the road on commencing a journey, and we see here that it was offered also in connexion with the king's going to the ancestral temple or the border altar.
3. It does not appear clearly what sacrifices the poet had in view here. I think they must be all those in which the kings of Kâu appeared as the principals or sacrificers. The concluding line is understood to intimate that the kings were not to forget that a prosperous agriculture was the foundation of their prosperity.
4. In this stanza we have the peculiar honour paid to Kâu-kî by his descendants at one of the great border sacrifices to God,—the same to which the last ode in the first decade of the Sacrificial Odes of Kau belongs.

king, at the close of the sacrifice in the ancestral temple, to the princes of his own surname. There are difficulties in the interpretation of the piece on this view, which, however, is to be preferred to any other.

In thick patches are those rushes, Springing by the wayside:—Let not the cattle and sheep trample them. Anon they will grow up; anon they will be completely formed, With their leaves soft and glossy[1]. Closely related are brethren; Let none be absent, let all be near. For some there are mats spread; For some there are given Stools [2].

The mats are spread, and a second one above; The stools are given, and there are plenty of servants. (The guests) are pledged, and they pledge (the host) in return; He rinses the cups (and refills them, but the guests) put them down, Sauces and pickles are brought in, With roasted meat and broiled. Excellent provisions there are of tripe and palates; With singing to lutes, and with drums.

The ornamented bows are strong, And the four arrows are all balanced. They discharge the arrows, and all hit, And the guests are arranged according to their skill. The ornamented bows are drawn to the full, And the arrows are grasped in the hand. They go straight to the mark as if planted

1. In the rushes growing up densely from a common root we have an emblem of brothers all sprung from the same ancestor; and in the plants developing. so finely, when preserved from injury, an emblem of the happy fellowships of consanguinity, when nothing is allowed to interfere with mutual confidence and good, feeling.
2. In a previous note I have said that chairs and tables had not come into use in those early times. Guests sat and feasts were spread on mats on the floor; for the aged, however, stools were. placed on which they could lean forward.

in it, And the guests are arranged according to the humble propriety of their behaviour.

The distant descendant presides over the feast; His sweet spirits are strong. He fills their cups from a large vase, And prays for the hoary old (among his guests):—That with hoary age and wrinkled back, They may lead on one another (to virtue), and' support one another (in it); That so their old age may be blessed, And their bright happiness ever increased.

ODE 3. THE KÎ ZUI.

RESPONSIVE TO THE LAST:—THE UNCLES AND BRETHREN OF THE KING EXPRESS THEIR SENSE OF HIS KINDNESS, AND THEIR WISHES FOR HIS HAPPINESS, MOSTLY IN THE WORDS IN WHICH THE PERSONATORS OF THE DEPARTED ANCESTORS HAD CONVEYED THEIR SATISFACTION WITH THE SACRIFICE OFFERED TO THEM, AND PROMISED TO HIM THEIR BLESSING.

You have made us drink to the full of your spirit; You have satiated us with your kindness. May you enjoy, O our lord, myriads of years! May your bright happiness (ever) be increased!

You have made us drink to the full of your spirits; Your viands were set out before us. May you enjoy, O our lord, myriads of years! May your bright intelligence ever be increased!

May your bright intelligence become perfect, High and brilliant, leading to a good end! That good end has (now) its beginning:—The personators of your ancestors announced it in their blessing.

What was their announcement? '(The offerings) in your dishes of bamboo and wood are clean and fine. Your friends [1], assisting in the service, Have done their part with reverent demeanour.

'Your reverent demeanour was altogether what the occasion required; And also that of your filial son [2]. For such filial piety, continued without ceasing, There will ever be conferred blessings upon you.'

What will the blessings be? 'That along the passages of your palace, You shall move for ten thousand years, And there will be granted to you for ever dignity and posterity.'

How as to your posterity? 'Heaven invests you with your dignity; Yea, for ten thousand years, The bright appointment is attached (to your line).'

How is it attached? 'There is given you a heroic wife. There is given you a heroic wife, And from her shall come the (line of) descendants.'

ODE 4. THE HÛ Î.

AN ODE APPROPRIATE TO THE FEAST GIVEN TO THE PERSONATORS OF THE DEPARTED, ON THE DAY AFTER THE SACRIFICE IN THE ANCESTRAL TEMPLE.

This supplementary sacrifice on the day after the principal service in the temple appeared in the ninth Book of the fourth Part of the Shû, and of the feast after it to the personators of the dead I have spoken on p. 301.

The wild-ducks and widgeons are on the King[3];

---

1. That is, the guests, visitors, and officers of the court.
2. Towards the end of the sacrificial service, the eldest son of the king joined in pledging the representatives of their ancestors.
3. The King is an affluent of the Wei, not far from Wû's capital of Hâo. The birds, feeling at home in its waters, on its sands, &c., serve to introduce the parties

feasted, in a situation where they might relax from the gravity of the preceding day, and be happy.

The personators of your ancestors feast and are happy. Your spirits are clear; Your viands are fragrant. The personators of your ancestors feast and drink;—Their happiness and dignity are made complete.

The wild-ducks and widgeons are on the sand; The personators of the dead enjoy the feast, their appropriate tribute. Your spirits are abundant; Your viands are good. The personators of your ancestors feast and drink;—Happiness and dignity lend them their aids.

The wild-ducks and widgeons are on the islets; The personators of your ancestors feast and enjoy themselves. Your spirits are strained; Your viands are in slices. The personators of your ancestors feast and drink;—Happiness and dignity descend on them.

The wild-ducks and widgeons are where the waters meet; The personators of your ancestors feast and are honoured. The feast is spread in the ancestral temple. The place where happiness and dignity descend. The personators of your ancestors feast and drink;—Their happiness and dignity are at the highest point.

The wild-ducks and widgeons are in the gorge; The personators of your ancestors rest, full of complacency. The fine spirits are delicious; Your meat, roast and broiled, is fragrant. The personators of your ancestors feast and drink;—No troubles will be theirs after this.

ODE 5, STANZA 1. THE KIÂ LO.

IN PRAISE OF SOME KING, WHOSE VIRTUE SECURED TO HIM THE FAVOUR OF HEAVEN.

Perhaps the response of the feasted personators of the ancestors.

Of our admirable, amiable sovereign Most illustrious is the excellent virtue. He orders rightly the people, orders rightly the officers, And receives his dignity from Heaven, Which protects and helps him, and (confirms) his appointment, By repeated acts of renewal from heaven.

ODE 8. THE KHÜAN Â.

ADDRESSED, PROBABLY, BY THE DUKE OF SHÂO TO KING KHANG, DESIRING FOR HIM LONG PROSPERITY, AND CONGRATULATING HIM, IN ORDER TO ADMONISH HIM, ON THE HAPPINESS OF HIS PEOPLE, THE NUMBER OF HIS ADMIRABLE OFFICERS, AND THE AUSPICIOUS OMEN ARISING FROM THE APPEARANCE OF THE PHŒNIX.

The duke of Shâo was the famous Shih, who appears in the fifth and other Books of the fifth Part of the Shû, the colleague of the duke of Kin in the early days of the Kâu dynasty. This piece may have been composed by him, but there is no evidence in it that it was so. The assigning it to him rests entirely on the authority of the preface. The language, however, is that in which an old statesman of that time might express his complacency in his young sovereign.

Into the recesses of the large mound Came the wind, whirling from the south. There was (our) happy, courteous sovereign, Rambling and singing; And I took occasion to give forth my notes.

'Full of spirits you ramble; Full of satisfaction you rest. O happy and courteous sovereign, May you fulfil your years, And end them like your ancestors!'

'Your territory is great and glorious, And perfectly secure. O happy and courteous sovereign, May you fulfil your years, As the host of all the spirits[1]!

'You have received the appointment long acknowledged, With peace around your happiness and dignity. O happy and courteous sovereign, May you fulfil your years, With pure happiness your constant possession!

'You have helpers and supporters, Men of filial piety and' of virtue, To lead you on, and act as wings to you, (So that), O happy and courteous sovereign, You are a pattern to the four quarters (of the kingdom).

Full of dignity and majesty (are they), Like a

1. 'Host of the hundred—i.e., of all—the spirits' is one of the titles of the sovereign of China. It was and is his prerogative to offer the great 'border sacrifices' to Heaven and Earth, or, as Confucius explains. them, to God, and to the spirits of his ancestors in his ancestral temple; and in his progresses (now neglected), among the states, to the spirits of the hills and 'rivers throughout the kingdom. Every feudal prince could only sacrifice to the hills and streams within his own territory. Under the changed conditions of the government of China, the sacrificial ritual of the emperor still retains the substance of whatever belonged to the sovereigns in this respect from the earliest dynasties. On the text here, Khung Ying-tâ of the Thang dynasty said, 'He who possesses all under the sky, sacrifices to all the spirits, and thus he is the host of them all.' Kû Hsî said on it, 'And always be the host of (the spirits of) Heaven and Earth, of the hills and rivers, and of the departed.' The term 'host' does not imply any superiority of rank on the part of the entertainer. In the greatest sacrifices the emperor acknowledges himself as 'the servant or subject of Heaven.' See the prayer of the first of the present Manchâu line of emperors, in announcing that he had ascended the throne, at the altar of Heaven and Earth, in 1644, as translated by the Rev. Dr. Edkins in the chapter on Imperial Worship, in the recent edition of his 'Religion in China.'

jade-mace(in its purity), The subject of praise, the contemplation of hope. O happy and courteous sovereign, (Through them) the four quarters (of the kingdom) are guided by you.

'The male and female phœnix fly about [1], Their wings rustling, While they settle in their proper resting-place. Many are your admirable officers, O king, Ready to be employed by you, Loving you, the Son of Heaven.

'The male and female phœnix fly about, Their wings rustling, As they soar up to heaven. Many are your admirable officers, O king, Waiting for your commands, And loving the multitudes of the people, The male and female phœnix give out their notes, On that lofty ridge. The dryandras grow, On those eastern slopes. They grow luxuriantly; And harmoniously the notes resound.

1. The phœnix (so the creature has been named) is a fabulous bird, 'the chief of the 360 classes of the winged tribes.' It is mentioned in the fourth Book of the second Part of the Shû, as appearing in the courtyard of Shun; and the appearance of a pair of them has always been understood to denote a sage on the throne and prosperity in the country. Even Confucius (Analects, IX, viii) could not express his hopelessness about his own times more strongly than by saying that 'the phœnix did not make its appearance.' He was himself also called 'a phœnix,' in derision, by one of the recluses of his time (Analects, XVIII, v). The type of' the bird

was, perhaps, the Argus pheasant, but the descriptions of it are of a monstrous creature, having' a fowl's head, a swallow's chin, a serpent's neck, a fish's tail,' &c. It only lights on the dryandra cordifolia, of which tree also many marvellous stories are related. The poet is not to be understood as saying that the phœnix actually appeared; but that the king was Âge and his government prosperous, as if it had appeared.

'Your chariots, O sovereign, Are numerous, many. Your horses, O sovereign, Are well trained and fleet. I have made my few verses, In prolongation of your song.'

ODE 9, STANZA 1. THE MIN LÂO.

IN A TIME OF DISORDER AND SUFFERING, SOME OFFICER OF DISTINCTION CALLS ON HIS FELLOWS TO JOIN WITH HIM TO EFFECT A REFORMATION IN THE CAPITAL, AND PUT AWAY THE PARTIES WHO WERE THE CAUSE OF THE PREVAILING MISERY.

With the Khüan Â, what are called the 'correct' odes of Part III, or those belonging to a period of good government, and the composition of which is ascribed mainly to the duke of Kâu, come to an end; and those that follow are the 'changed' Major Odes of the Kingdom, or those belonging to a degenerate period, commencing with this. Some among them, however, are equal to any of the former class. The Min Lâo has been assigned to duke Mû of Shâo, a descendant of duke Khang, the Shih of the Shû, the reputed author of the Khüan Â, and was directed against king Lî, B.C. 878 to 828.

The people indeed are heavily burdened, But perhaps a little relief may be got for them. Let us cherish this centre of the kingdom, To secure the repose of the four quarters of it. Let us give no indulgence to the wily and obsequious, In order to make the unconscientious careful, And to repress robbers and oppressors, Who have no fear of the clear will (of Heaven)[1]. Then let us show kindness to those who are distant, And help those who are near,— Thus establishing (the throne of) our king.

1. 'The clear will,' according to Kû Hsî, is 'the clear appointment of Heaven;' according to Kû Kung-khien, 'correct principle.' They both mean the law of human duty, as gathered from the nature of man's moral constitution conferred by Heaven.

ODE 10. THE PAN.

AN OFFICER OF EXPERIENCE MOURNS OVER THE PREVAILING MISERY; COMPLAINS OF THE WANT OF SYMPATHY WITH HIM SHOWN BY OTHER OFFICERS; ADMONISHES THEM, AND SETS FORTH THE DUTY REQUIRED OF THEM, ESPECIALLY IN THE ANGRY MOOD IN WHICH IT MIGHT SEEM THAT HEAVEN WAS.

This piece, like the last, is assigned to the time of king Lî.

God has reversed (his usual course of procedure)[1], And the lower people are full of distress. The words which you utter are not right; The plans which you form are not far-reaching. As there are not sages, you think you have no guidance;—You have no real sincerity. (Thus) your plans do not reach far, And I therefore strongly admonish you.

Heaven is now sending down calamities;—Do not be so complacent. Heaven is now producing such movements;—Do not be so indifferent. If your words were harmonious, The people would become united. If your words were gentle and kind, The people would be settled.

Though my duties are different from yours, I am your fellow-servant. I come to advise with you, And you hear me with contemptuous indifference, My words are about the (present urgent) affairs;—Do not think them matter for laughter. The ancients had a saying:—'Consult the gatherers of grass and firewood[2].'

1. The proof of God's having reversed his usual course of procedure was to be found in the universal misery of the people, whose good He was understood to desire, and for the securing of which government by, righteous kings was maintained by him.
2. If ancient worthies thought that persons in such mean employments were to he consulted surely, the advice of the writer deserved to be taken into account by his comrades.

Heaven is now exercising oppression;—Do not in such a way make a mock of things. An old man, (I speak) with entire sincerity; But you, my juniors, are full of pride. It is not that my words are those of age, But you make a joke of what is sad. But the troubles will multiply like flames, Till they are beyond help or remedy.

Heaven is now displaying its anger;—Do not be either boastful or flattering, Utterly departing from all propriety of demeanour, Till good men are reduced to personators of the dead [1]. The people now sigh and groan, And we dare not examine (into the causes of their trouble). The ruin and disorder are exhausting all their means of living, And we show no kindness to our multitudes.

Heaven enlightens the people [2], As the bamboo flute responds to the earthen whistle; As two half-maces form a whole one; As you take a thing, and bring it away in your hand, Bringing it away, without any more ado. The enlightenment of the people is very easy. They have (now) many perversities;—Do not you set up your perversity before them.

Good men are a fence; The multitudes of the people are a wall; Great states are screens; Great families are buttresses;—The cherishing of virtue

1. During all the time of the sacrifice, the personators of the dead said not a word, but only ate and drank. To the semblance of them good men were now reduced.
2. The meaning is, that Heaven has so attuned the mind to virtue, that, if good example were set before the people, they would certainly and readily follow it. This is illustrated by various instances of things, in which the one succeeded the other freely and as it necessarily; so that government by virtue was really very easy.

secures repose; The circle of (the king's) relatives is a fortified wall. We must not let the fortified wall get destroyed; We must not let (the king) be solitary and consumed with terrors.

Revere the anger of Heaven, And presume not to make sport or be idle. Revere the changing moods of Heaven, And presume not to drive about (at your pleasure). Great Heaven is intelligent, And is with you in all your goings. Great Heaven is clear-seeing, And is with you in your wanderings and indulgences.

The Third Decade, or that of Tang.

ODE 1. THE TANG.

WARNINGS, SUPPOSED TO BE ADDRESSED TO KING LÎ, ON THE ISSUES OF THE COURSE WHICH HE WAS PURSUING, SHOWING THAT THE MISERIES OF THE TIME AND THE IMMINENT DANGER OF RUIN WERE TO BE ATTRIBUTED, NOT TO HEAVEN, BUT TO HIMSELF AND HIS MINISTERS.

This ode, like the ninth of the second decade, is attributed to duke Mû of Shâo. The structure of the piece is peculiar, for, after the first stanza, we have king Wǎn introduced delivering a series of warnings to Kâu-hsin, the last king of the Shang dynasty. They are put into Wǎn's mouth, in the hope that Lî, if, indeed, he was the monarch whom the writer had in view, would transfer the figure of Kâu-hsin to himself, and alter his course so as to avoid a similar ruin.

How vast is God, The ruler of men below! How arrayed in terrors is God, With many things irregular in his ordinations. Heaven gave birth to the multitudes of the people, But the nature it confers is not to be depended on. All are (good) at first, But few prove themselves to be so at the last[1].

King Wan said, 'Alas! Alas! you sovereign of Shang, That you should have such violently oppressive ministers, That you should have such extortionate exactors, That you should have them in offices, That you should have them in the conduct of affairs! "Heaven made them with their insolent dispositions;" But it is you who employ them, and give them strength.'

King Wan said, 'Alas! Alas! you (sovereign of) Yin-shang, You ought to employ such as are good, But (you employ instead) violent oppressors, who cause many dissatisfactions. They respond to you with baseless stories, And (thus) robbers and thieves are in your court. Hence come oaths and curses, Without limit, without end.'

King Wan said, 'Alas! Alas! you (sovereign of) Yin-shang, You show a strong fierce will in the centre of the kingdom, And consider the contracting of enmities a proof of virtue. All-unintelligent are you. Of your (proper) virtue, And so, you have no (good) men behind you, nor by your side. Without any intelligence of your (proper) virtue, You have no (good) intimate adviser or minister.'

King Wan said, 'Alas! Alas! you (sovereign of) Yin-shang, It is not Heaven that flushes your face with spirits, So that you follow what is evil and imitate it. You go wrong in all your conduct; You make no distinction between the light and the

1. The meaning seems to be that, whatever miseries might prevail, and be ignorantly ascribed to God, they were in reality owing to men's neglect of the law of Heaven inscribed on their hearts.

darkness; But amid clamour and shouting, You turn the day into night[1].'

King Wan said, 'Alas! Alas! you (sovereign of) Yin-shang, (All round you) is like the noise of cicadas, Or like the bubbling of boiling soup. Affairs, great and small, are approaching to ruin, And still you (and your creatures) go on in this course. Indignation is rife against you here in the Middle Kingdom, And extends to the demon regions [2].'

King Wan said, 'Alas! Alas! you (sovereign of) Yin-shang, It is not God that has caused this evil time, But it arises from Yin's not using the old (ways). Although you have not old experienced men, There are still the ancient statutes and laws. But you will not listen to them, And so your great appointment is being overthrown.'

King Wan said, 'Alas! Alas! you (sovereign of) Shang, People have a saying, "When a tree falls utterly, While its branches and leaves are yet uninjured, It must first have been uprooted." The beacon of Yin is not far distant;—It is in the age of the (last) sovereign of Hsiâ.'

1. We speak of 'turning night into day.' The tyrant of Shang turned day into night, Excesses, generally committed in darkness, were by him done openly.
2. These 'demon regions' are understood to mean the seat of the Turkic tribes to the north of China, known from the earliest times by various names-'The hill Zung,' 'the northern Lî,' 'the Hsien-yun,' &c. Towards the beginning of our era, they were called Hsiung-nû, from which, perhaps, came the name Huns; and some centuries later, Thû-küeh (Thuh-küeh), from which came Turk. We are told in the Yî, under the diagram Kî-kî, that Kâo Zung (B.C. 1324-1266) conducted an expedition against the demon regions, and in three years subdued them

ODE 2. THE YÎ.

CONTAINING VARIOUS COUNSELS WHICH DUKE WÛ OF WEI MADE TO ADMONISH HIMSELF, WHEN HE WAS OVER HIS NINETIETH YEAR; ESPECIALLY ON THE DUTY OF A RULER TO BE CAREFUL OF HIS OUTWARD DEMEANOUR, FEELING THAT HE IS EVER UNDER THE INSPECTION OF SPIRITUAL BEINGS, AND TO RECEIVE WITH DOCILITY INSTRUCTIONS DELIVERED TO HIM.

The sixth ode in the seventh decade of the Minor Odes of the Kingdom is attributed to the same duke of Wei as this; and the two bear traces of having proceeded from the same writer. The external authorities for assigning this piece to duke Wû are the statement of the preface and an article in the 'Narratives of the States,' a work already referred to as belonging to the period of the Kâu dynasty. That article relates how Wû, at the age of ninety-five, insisted on all his ministers and officers being instant, in season and out of season, to admonish him on his conduct, and that 'he made the warnings in the Î to admonish himself.' The Î is understood to be only another name for this Yî. Thus the speaker throughout the piece is Wû, and 'the young Son,' whom he sometimes addresses, is himself also. The conception of the writer in taking such a method to admonish himself, and give forth the lessons of his long life, is very remarkable; and the execution of it is successful.

Outward demeanour, cautious and grave, Is an indication of the (inward) virtue. People have the saying, 'There is no wise man who is not (also) stupid.' The stupidity of the ordinary man Is determined by his (natural) defects. The stupidity of the wise man Is from his doing violence (to his proper character).

What is most powerful is the being the man [1];—

1. Wû writes as the marquis of Wei, the ruler of a state; but what he says is susceptible of universal application. In every smaller sphere, and in the largest, 'being the man,' displaying, that is, the proper qualities of humanity, will be appreciated and felt.

In all quarters (of the state) men are influenced by it. To an upright virtuous conduct All in the four quarters of the state render obedient homage. With great counsels and determinate orders, With far-reaching plans and timely announcements, And with reverent care of his outward demeanour, One will become the pattern of the people.

As for the circumstances of the present time, You are bent on error and confusion in your government. Your virtue is subverted; You are besotted by drink [1]. Although you thus pursue nothing but pleasure, How is it you do not think of your relation to the past, And do not widely study the former kings, That you might hold fast their wise laws?

Shall not those whom great Heaven does not approve of, Surely as the waters flow from a spring, Sink down together in ruin? Rise early and go to bed late, Sprinkle and sweep your courtyard;— So as to be a pattern to the people [2]. Have in good order your chariots and horses, Your bows and arrows, and (other) weapons of war;—To be prepared for warlike action, To keep at a distance (the hordes of) the south.

Perfect what concerns your officers and people;

1. Han Ying (who has been mentioned in the Introduction) says that Wû made the sixth ode of the seventh decade of the former Part against drunkenness, when he was repenting of his own giving way to that vice. His mention of the habit here, at the age of ninety-five, must be understood as a warning to other rulers.
2. Line 3 describes things important to the cultivation of one's self; and line 4, things important to the regulation of one's family. They may seem unimportant, it is said,.. as compared with the defence of the state, spoken of in the last four lines of the stanza; but the ruler ought not to neglect them.

Be careful of your duties as a prince (of the kingdom). To be prepared for unforeseen dangers, Be cautious of what you say; Be reverentially careful of your outward behaviour; In all things be mild and correct. A flaw in a mace of white jade May be ground away; But for a flaw in speech Nothing can be done.

Do not speak lightly; your words are your own[1]. Do not say, 'This is of little importance; No one can hold my tongue for me.' Words are not to be cast away. Every word finds its answer; Every good deed has its recompense. If you are gracious among your friends, And to the people, as if they were your children, Your descendants will continue in unbroken line, And all the people will surely be obedient to you.

Looked at in friendly intercourse with superior men, You make your countenance harmonious and mild; Anxious not to do anything wrong. Looked at in your chamber, You ought to be equally free from shame before the light which shines in. Do not say, 'This place is not public; No one can see me here.' The approaches of spiritual beings Cannot be calculated beforehand; But the more should they not be slighted [2].

1. And therefore every one is himself responsible for his words.
2. Kû Hsî says that from the fourth line this stanza only speaks of the constant care there should be in watching over one's thoughts; but in saying so, be overlooks the consideration by which such watchful care is enforced. Compare what is said of king Wan in the third stanza of the sixth ode of the first decade. King Wan and duke Wû were both influenced by the consideration that their inmost thoughts, even when 'unseen by men,' were open to the inspection of spiritual beings.

O prince, let your practice of virtue Be entirely good and admirable. Watch well over your behaviour, And allow nothing wrong in your demeanour. Committing no excess, doing nothing injurious, There are few who will not in such a case take you for their pattern. When one throws to me a peach, I return to him a plum [1]. To look for horns on a young ram Will only weary you, my son [2].

The tough and elastic wood Can be fitted with the silken string [3]. The mild and respectful man Possesses the foundation of virtue. There is a wise man;—I tell him good words, And he yields to them the practice of docile virtue. There is a stupid man;—He says on the contrary that my words are not true:—So different are people's minds.

Oh! my son, When you did not know what was good, and what was not good, Not only did I lead you by the hand, But I showed the difference between them by appealing to instances. Not (only) did I charge you face to face, But I held you by the ear [4]. And still perhaps you do not know, Although you have held a son in your arms. If people be not self-sufficient, Who comes to a late maturity after early instruction?

Great Heaven is very intelligent, And I pass,

1. That is, every deed, in fact, meets with its recompense.

2. See the conclusion of duke Wû's ode against drunkenness. Horns grow as the young ram grows. Effects must not be expected where there have not been the conditions from which they naturally spring.
3. Such wood is the proper material for a bow.
4. That is, to secure your attention.

my life without pleasure. When I see you so dark and stupid, My heart is full of pain. I taught you with assiduous repetition, And you listened to me with contempt. You would not consider me as your teacher, But regarded me as troublesome. Still perhaps you do not know;—But you are very old.

Oh! my son, I have told you the old ways. Hear and follow my counsels:—Then shall you have no cause for great regret. Heaven is now inflicting calamities, And is destroying the state. My illustrations are not taken from things remote:—Great Heaven makes no mistakes. If you go on to deteriorate in your virtue, You will bring the people to great distress.

ODE 3, STANZAS 1, 2, 3, 4, AND 7. THE SANG ZÂU.

THE WRITER MOURNS OVER THE MISERY AND DISORDER OF THE TIMES, WITH A VIEW TO REPREHEND THE MISGOVERNMENT OF KING LÎ, APPEALING ALSO TO HEAVEN TO HAVE COMPASSION.

King Lî is not mentioned by name in the piece, but the second line of stanza 7 can only be explained of him. He was driven from the throne, in consequence of his misgovernment, in B.C. 842, and only saved his life by flying to Kih, a place in the present Ho Kâu, department Phing-yang, Shan-hsî, where he remained till his death in B.C. 828. The government in the meantime was carried on by the dukes of Shâo and Kâu, whose administration, called the period of 'Mutual Harmony,' forms an important chronological era in Chinese history. On the authority of a reference in the Zo Kwan, the piece is ascribed to an earl of Zui.

Luxuriant is that young mulberry tree, And beneath it wide is the shade; But they will pluck its leaves till it is quite destroyed[1]. The distress

1. These three lines are metaphorical of the once flourishing kingdom, which was now brought to the verge of ruin.

inflicted on these (multitudes of the) people, Is an unceasing sorrow to my heart; My commiseration fills (my breast). O thou bright and great Heaven, Shouldest thou not have compassion on us?

The four steeds (gallop about), eager and strong[1]; The tortoise-and-serpent and the falcon banners fly about. Disorder grows, and no peace can be secured. Every state is being ruined; There are no black heads among the people[2]. Everything is reduced to ashes by calamity. Oh! alas! The doom of the kingdom hurries on.

There is nothing to arrest the doom of the kingdom; Heaven does not nourish us. There is no place in which to stop securely; There is no place to which to go. Superior men are the bonds (Of the social state)[3], Allowing no love of strife in their hearts. Who reared the steps of the dissatisfaction [4], Which has reached the present distress?

The grief of my heart is extreme, And I dwell on (the condition of) our land. I was born at an unhappy time, To meet with the severe anger of Heaven. From the west to the east, There is no quiet place of abiding. Many are the distresses I meet with; Very urgent is the trouble on our borders.

Heaven is sending down death and disorder, And

1. That is, the war-chariots, each drawn by its team of four horses.
2. The young and able-bodied of the people were slain or absent on distant expeditions, and only old and gray-headed men were to be seen.
3. Intimating that no such men were now to be found in office.
4. Meaning the king by his misgovernment and employment of bad men.

has put an end to our king. It is (now) sending down those devourers of the grain, So that the husbandry is all in evil case. Alas for our middle states [1]! All is in peril and going to ruin. I have no strength (to do anything), And think of (the Power in) the azure vault.

ODE 4. THE YUN HAN.

KING HSÜAN, ON OCCASION OF A GREAT DROUGHT, EXPOSTULATES WITH GOD AND ALL THE SPIRITS, WHO MIGHT BE EXPECTED TO HELP HIM AND HIS PEOPLE; ASKS THEM WHEREFORE THEY WERE CONTENDING WITH HIM; AND DETAILS THE MEASURES HE HAD TAKEN, AND WAS STILL TAKING, FOR THE REMOVAL OF THE CALAMITY.

King Hsüan does not occur by name in the ode, though the remarkable prayer which it relates is ascribed to a king in stanza 1. All critics have admitted the statement of the Preface that the piece was made, in admiration of king Hsüan, by Zang Shû, a great officer, we may presume, of the court. The standard chronology places the commencement of the drought in B.C. 822, the sixth year of Hsüan's reign. How long it continued we cannot tell.

Bright was the milky way, Shining and revolving in the sky. The king said, 'Oh! What crime is chargeable on us now, That Heaven (thus) sends down death and disorder? Famine comes again and again. There is no spirit I have not sacrificed to[2]; There is no victim I have grudged; Our

1. We must translate here in the plural, 'the middle states' meaning all the states subject to the sovereign of Kâu.
2. In the Official Book of Kâu, among the duties of the Minister of Instruction, or, as Biot translates the title, 'the Director of the Multitudes,' it is stated that one of the things he has to do, on occurrences of famine, is 'to seek out the spirits,' that is, as explained by the commentators, to see that sacrifices are offered to all the spirits, even such as may have been discontinued. This rule had, no doubt, been acted on during the drought which this ode describes.

jade symbols, oblong and round, are exhausted[1];— How is it that I am not heard?

'The drought is excessive; Its fervours become more and more tormenting. I have not ceased offering pure sacrifices; From the border altars I have gone to the ancestral temple [2]. To the (Powers) above and below I have presented my offerings and then' buried them[3];—There is no spirit whom I have not honoured. Hâu-kî is not equal to the occasion; God does not come to us. This wasting and ruin of our country,—Would that it fell (only) on me!

'The drought is excessive, And I may not try to excuse myself. I am full of terror, and feel the peril, Like the clap of thunder or the roll. Of the remnant of Kâu, among the black-haired people, There will not be half a man left; Nor will God from his great heaven exempt (even) me. Shall

1. We have, in the sixth Book of the fifth Part of the Shû, an instance of the use of the symbols here mentioned in sacrificing to the spirits of departed kings. The Official Book, among the duties of the Minister of Religion, mentions the use of these and other symbols—in all six, of different shapes and colours—at the different sacrifices.
2. By 'the border altars' we are to understand the altars in the suburbs of the capital, where Heaven and Earth were sacrificed to -the great services at the solstices, and any other seasons. The mention of Hâu-kî in the seventh line makes us think especially of the service in the spring, to pray for a good year, when Hâu-kî was associated with God.
3. 'The (Powers) above and below' are Heaven and Earth. The offerings, during the progress of the service, were placed on the ground, or on the altars, and buried in the earth at the close of it. This explains what the king says in the first stanza about the offerings of jade being exhausted.

we not mingle our fears together? (The sacrifices to) my ancestors will be extinguished[1].

'The drought is excessive, And it -cannot be stopped. More fierce and fiery, It is leaving me no place. My end is near;—I have none to look up, none to look round, to. The many dukes and their ministers of the past [2] Give me no help. O ye parents and (nearer) ancestors [3], How can ye bear to see me thus?

'The drought is excessive;—Parched are the hills, and the streams are dried. The demon of drought exercises his oppression, As if scattering flames and fire [4] My heart is terrified with the heat;—My sorrowing heart is as if on fire. The

1. Equivalent to the extinction of the dynasty.
2. The king had sacrificed to all the early lords of Kâu. 'The many dukes' may comprehend kings Thâi and Kî. He had also sacrificed to their ministers. Compare what Pan-kang says in the Shû, p. 109, about his predecessors and their ministers. Some take 'the many dukes, and the ministers,' of all princes of states who had signalised themselves by services to the people and kingdom.
3. The king could hardly hope that his father, the oppressive Lî, would in his spirit-state give him any aid; but we need only find in his words the expression of natural feeling. Probably it was the consideration of the character of Lî which has made some critics understand by 'parents' and 'ancestors' the same individuals, namely,

4. Khung Ying-tâ, from 'the Book of Spirits and Marvels,' gives the following account of 'the demon of drought:'—'In the southern regions there is a man, two or three cubits in height, with the upper part of his body bare, and his eyes in the top of his head. He runs with the speed of the wind, and is named Po. In whatever state he appears, there ensues a great drought.' The Book of Spirits and Marvels, however, as it now exists, cannot be older, than our fourth or fifth century.

many dukes and their ministers of the past Do not hear me. O God, from thy great heaven, Grant me the liberty to withdraw (into retirement[1]).

'The drought is excessive;—I struggle and fear to go away. How is it that I am afflicted with this drought? I cannot ascertain the cause of it. In praying for a good year I was abundantly early [2]. I was not late (in sacrificing) to (the spirits of) the four quarters and of the land [3]. God in great heaven Does not consider me. Reverent to the intelligent spirits, I ought not to be thus the object of their anger.

'The drought is excessive;—All is dispersion, and the bonds of government are relaxed. Reduced to extremities are the heads of departments; Full of distress are my chief ministers, The Master of the Horse, the Commander of the Guards, The chief Cook[4], and my attendants. There is no one who has not (tried to) help (the people); They have not refrained on the ground of being unable. I look up to the great heaven;—Why am I plunged in this sorrow?

'I look up to the great heaven, But its stars sparkle bright. My great officers and excellent men, Ye have reverently drawn near (to Heaven) with all

1. That is, to withdraw and give place to a more worthy sovereign.
2. This was the border sacrifice to God, when Hâu-kî was associated with him. Some critics add a sacrifice in -the first month of winter, for a blessing on the ensuing year, offered to 'the honoured ones of heaven,'—the sun, moon, and zodiacal constellations.
3. See note 2 on p. 371.
4. See note 1 On p. 356.

your powers. Death is approaching, But do not cast away what you have done You are seeking not for me only, But to give rest to all our departments. I look up to the great heaven;—When shall I be favoured with repose?'

ODE 5, STANZAS 1, 2, AND 4. THE SUNG KÂO.

CELEBRATING THE APPOINTMENT BY KING HSÜAN OF A RELATIVE TO BE THE MARQUIS OF SHAN, AND DEFENDER OF THE SOUTHERN BORDER OF THE KINGDOM, WITH THE ARRANGEMENTS MADE FOR HIS ENTERING ON HIS CHARGE.

That the king who appears in this piece was king Hsüan is sufficiently established. He appears in it commissioning 'his great uncle,' an elder brother, that is, of his mother, to go and rule, as marquis of Shan, and chief or president of the states in the south of the kingdom, to defend the borders against the encroaching hordes of the south, headed by the princes of Khû, whose lords bad been rebellious against the middle states even in the time of the Shang dynasty;—see the last of the Sacrificial Odes of Shang.

Grandly lofty are the mountains, With their large masses reaching to the heavens. From those mountains was sent down a spirit, Who produced the birth of (the princes of) Fû and Shan [1]. Fû and

1. Shan was a small marquisate, a part of what is the present department of Nan-yang, Ho-nan. Fû, which was also called Lü, was another small territory, not far from Shan. The princes of both were Kiangs, descended from the chief minister of Yâo, called in the first Book of the Shû, 'the Four Mountains.' Other states were ruled by his descendants, particularly the great state of Khî. When it is said here that a spirit was sent down from the great mountains, and produced the birth of (the princes of) Fû and Shan, we have, probably, a legendary tradition concerning the birth of Yâo's minister, which was current among all his descendants; and with which we may compare the legends that have come under our notice about the supernatural births of the ancestors of the founders of the Houses of Shang and Kau. The character for mountains' in lines 1 and 3 is the same that occurs in the title of Yâo's minister. On the statement about the mountains sending 'down a spirit, Hwang Hsün, a critic of the Sung dynasty, says that it is merely a personification of the poet, to show how high Heaven had a mind to revive the fortunes of Kau, and that we need not trouble ourselves about whether there was such a spirit or not!

Shan Are the support of Kâu, Screens to all the states, Diffusing (their influence) over the four quarters of the kingdom.

Full of activity is the chief of Shin, And the king would employ him to continue the services (of his fathers), With his capital in Hsieh [1], Where he should be a pattern to the states of the south. The king gave charge to the earl of Shâo, To arrange all about the residence of the chief of Shin, Where he should do what was necessary for the regions of the south, And where his posterity might maintain his merit.

Of the services of the chief of Shan The foundation was laid by the earl of Shâo, Who first built the walls (of his city), And then completed his ancestral temple [2]. When the temple was completed, wide and grand, The king conferred on the chief of Shâo Four noble steeds, With the hooks for the trappings of the breast-bands, glittering bright [3].

1. Hsieh was in the present Fang Kâu of the department of Nan-yang.
2. Compare with this the account given, in ode 3 of the first decade, of the settling of 'the ancient duke Than-fû' in the plain of Kâu. Here, as there, the great religious edifice, the ancestral temple, takes precedence of all other buildings in the new city.
3. The steeds with their equipments were tokens of the royal favour, usually granted on occasions of investiture. The conferring of them was followed immediately by the departure of the newly-invested prince to his charge.

ODE 6, STANZAS 1 AND 7. THE KANG MIN.

CELEBRATING THE VIRTUES OF KUNG SHAN-FÛ, WHO APPEARS TO HAVE BEEN ONE OF THE PRINCIPAL MINISTERS OF KING HSÜAN, AND HIS DESPATCH TO THE EAST, TO FORTIFY THE CAPITAL OF TIM STATE OF KHÎ.

Heaven, in giving birth to the multitudes of the people, To every faculty and relationship annexed its law. The people possess this normal nature, And they (consequently) love its normal virtue [1] Heaven beheld the ruler of Kâu, Brilliantly affecting it by his conduct below, And to maintain him, its Son, Gave birth to Kung Shan-fû [2].

Kung Shan-fû went forth, having sacrificed to the spirit of the road [3]. His four steeds were strong;

1. We get an idea of the meaning which has been attached to these four lines from a very early time by Mencius' quotation of them (VI, i, ch. 6) in support of his

doctrine of the goodness of human nature, and the remark on the piece which he 'attributes to Confucius, that 'the maker of it knew indeed the constitution (of our nature).' Every faculty, bodily or mental, has its function to fulfil, and every relationship its duty to be discharged. The function and the duty are the things which the human being has to observe:—the seeing clearly, for instance, with the eyes, and bearing distinctly with the ears; the maintenance of righteousness between ruler and minister, and of affection between parent and child. This is the 'normal nature,' and the 'normal virtue' is the nature fulfilling the various laws of its constitution.

2   The connexion between these four lines and those that precede is this:—that while Heaven produces all men with the good nature there described, on occasions it produces others with virtue and powers in a super-eminent degree. Such an occasion was presented by the case of king Hsüan, and therefore, to mark its appreciation of him, and for his help, it now produced Kung Shan-fû.

3   This was a special sacrifice at the commencement of a journey, or of an expedition. See note 2 on p. 399.

His men were alert, He was always anxious lest he should not be equal to his commission; His steeds went on without stopping, To the tinkling of their eight bells. The king had given charge to Kung Shan-fû, To fortify the city there in the east.

ODE 7, STANZAS I AND PART OF 3. THE HAN YÎ.

CELEBRATING THE MARQUIS OF HAN:—HIS INVESTITURE, AND THE KING S CHARGE TO HIM; THE GIFTS HE RECEIVED, AND THE PARTING FEAST AT THE COURT; HIS MARRIAGE; THE EXCELLENCE OF HIS TERRITORY; AND HIS SWAY OVER THE REGIONS OF THE NORTH.

Only one line—the first of stanza 3—in this interesting piece serves to illustrate the religious practices of the time, and needs no further note than what has been given on the first line of stanza 7 in the preceding ode. The name of the marquisate of Han remains in the district of Han-khang, department of Hsî-an, Shen-hsî, in which also is mount Liang.

Very grand is the mountain of Liang, Which was made cultivable by Yü. Bright is the way from it, (Along which came) the marquis of Han to receive investiture. The king in person gave the charge:—'Continue the services of your ancestors; Let not my charge to you come to nought. Be diligent early and late, And reverently discharge your duties:—So shall my appointment of you not change. Be a support against those princes who do not come to court, Thus assisting your sovereign.'

When the marquis of Han left the court, he sacrificed to the spirit of the road. He went forth, and lodged for the night in Tû.

ODE 8, STANZAS 4 AND 5. THE KIANG HAN.

CELEBRATING AN EXPEDITION AGAINST THE SOUTHERN TRIBES OF THE HWÂI, AND THE WORK DONE FOR THE KING IN THEIR COUNTRY, BY HÛ, THE EARL OF SHÂO, WITH THE MANNER IN WHICH THE KING REWARDED HIM, AND HE RESPONDED TO THE ROYAL FAVOUR.

Hû was probably the same earl of Shâo, who is mentioned in ode 5, as building his capital of Hsieh for the new marquis of Shan. The lords of Shâo had been distinguished in the service of Kâu ever since the rise of the dynasty.

The king gave charge to Hû of Shâo:—'You have everywhere made known (and carried out my orders). When (the kings) Wan and Wû received their appointment, The duke of Shâo was their strong support. You not (only) have a regard to me the little child But you try to resemble that duke of Shâo. You have commenced and earnestly displayed your merit; And I will make you happy.

'I give you a large libation-cup of jade[1], And a jar of herb-flavoured spirits from the black millet[2]. I have made announcement to the Accomplished one[3], And confer on you hills, lands, and fields. In (Khî-)kâu shall you receive investiture, According as your ancestor received his.' Hû bowed with

1. See note 2 on p. 386.
2. The cup and the spirits would be used by the earl when sacrificing in his ancestral temple. Compare the similar gift from king Khang to the duke of Kâu, in the Shû, p. 194. More substantial gifts are immediately specified.
3. 'The Accomplished one' is understood to be king Wan (= 'the Accomplished king'). He was the founder of the Kâu dynasty. To him the kingdom had first come by the appointment and gift of Heaven. It was the duty therefore of his successors,

> in making grants of territory to meritorious officers, to announce them to him in Khî-kâu, the old territory of the family, and obtain, as it were, his leave for what they were doing.

his head to the ground (and said), 'May the Son of Heaven live for ever!'

ODE 10, STANZAS 1, 5, 6, AND 7. THE KAN ZANG.

THE WRITER DEPLORES, WITH AN APPEALING WAIL TO HEAVEN, THE MISERY AND OPPRESSION THAT PREVAILED, AND INTIMATES THAT THEY WERE CAUSED BY THE INTERFERENCE OF WOMEN AND EUNUCHS IN THE GOVERNMENT.

The king addressed in this piece was most probably Yû. It suits his character and reign.

I look up to great Heaven, But it shows us no kindness. Very long have we been disquieted, And these great calamities are sent down (upon us). There is nothing settled in the country; Officers and people are in distress. Through the insects from without and from within, There is no peace or limit (to our misery). The net of crime is not taken up[1], And there is no peace nor cure (for our state).

Why is it that Heaven is (thus) reproving (you)? Why is it that Heaven is not blessing (you)? You neglect your great barbarian (foes), And regard me with hatred. You are regardless of the evil omens (that abound [2]), And your demeanour is all unseemly. (Good) men are going away, And the country is sure to go to ruin.

Heaven is letting down its net, And many (are the calamities in it). (Good) men are going away, And my heart is sorrowful. Heaven is letting down

1. By 'the net of crime' we are to understand the multitude of penal laws, to whose doom people were exposed. In stanza 6, Heaven is represented as letting it down.
2. Compare ode 9 of the fourth decade in the former Part.

its net, And soon (all will be caught in it). (Good) men are going away, And my heart is sad.

Right from the spring comes the water bubbling, Revealing its depth. The sorrow of my heart,—Is it (only) of to-day? Why were these things not, before me? Or why were they not after me? But mysteriously great Heaven Is able to strengthen anything. Do not disgrace your great ancestors This will save your posterity[1].

ODE 11, STANZAS 1 AND 2. THE SHÂO MIN.

THE WRITER APPEALS TO HEAVEN, BEMOANING THE MISERY AND RUIN WHICH WERE GOING ON, AND SHOWING HOW THEY WERE DUE TO THE KING'S EMPLOYMENT OF MEAN AND WORTHLESS CREATURES

Compassionate Heaven is arrayed in angry terrors. Heaven is indeed sending down ruin, Afflicting us with famine, So that the people are all wandering fugitives. In the settled regions, and on the borders, all is desolation.

Heaven sends down its net of crime;—Devouring insects, who weary and confuse men's minds, Ignorant, oppressive, negligent, Breeders of confusion, utterly perverse:—These are the men employed.

1. The writer in these concluding lines ventures to summon the king to repentance, and to hold out a hope that there might come a change in their state. He does this, believing that all things are possible with Heaven.

IV.

LESSONS FROM THE STATES.

ODES AND STANZAS ILLUSTRATING THE RELIGIOUS VIEWS AND PRACTICES OF THE WRITERS AND THEIR TIMES.

IT has been stated in the Introduction, p. 276, that the first Part of the Shih, called the Kwo Fang, or 'Lessons from the States,' consists of 160 pieces, descriptive of manners and events in several of the feudal states into which the kingdom of Kâu was divided. Nearly all of them are short; and the passages illustrating the religious views and practices of their times are comparatively few. What passages there are, however, of this nature will all be found below. The pieces are not arranged in decades, as in the Odes of the Kingdom, but in Books, under the names of the states in which they were produced.

Although the Kwo Fang form, as usually published, the first Part of the Shih, nearly all of them are more recent in their origin than the pieces of the other Parts. They bring us face to face with the states of the kingdom, and the ways of their officers and people for several centuries of the dynasty of Kâu.

BOOK II. THE ODES OF SHÂO AND THE SOUTH.

THE Shû and previous portions of the Shih have made us familiar with Shâo, the name of the appanage of Shih, one of the principal ministers at the court of Kâu in the first two reigns of the dynasty. The site of the city of Shâo was in the present department of Fang-khiang, Shen-hsî. The first possessor of it, along with the still more famous duke of Kâu, remained at court, to watch over the fortunes of the new dynasty. They were known as 'the highest dukes' and 'the two great chiefs,' the duke of Kâu having charge of the eastern portions of the kingdom, and the other of the western. The pieces in this Book are supposed to have been produced in Shâo, and the principalities south of it within his jurisdiction, by the duke.

ODE 2. THE ZHÂI FAN.

CELEBRATING THE INDUSTRY AND REVERENCE OF A PRINCE'S WIFE, ASSISTING HIM IN SACRIFICING.

We must suppose the ladies of a harem, in one Of the states of the south, admiring and praising in these simple stanzas the way in which their mistress discharged her duties. A view of the ode maintained by many is that the lady gathered the southernwood, not to use it in sacrificing, but in the nurture, of the silkworms under her care; but the evidence of the characters in the text is, on the whole, in favour of the more common view. Constant reference is made to the piece by Chinese moralists, to show that the most trivial things are accepted in sacrifice, when there are reverence and sincerity in the presenting of them.

One critic asked Kû Hsî whether it was conceivable that the wife of a prince did herself what is here related, and he replied that the poet said so. Another has observed that if the lady ordered and employed others, it was still her own doing. But that the lady did it herself is not incredible, when we consider the simplicity of those early times, in the twelfth century B.C.

She gathers the white southernwood, By the ponds, on the islets. She employs it, In the business of our prince.

She gathers the white southernwood, Along the streams in the valleys. She employs it, In the temple [1] of our prince.

1. If the character here translated 'temple' had no other signification but that, there would-be an end of the dispute about the meaning of the piece. But while we find

it often used- of the ancestral temple, it may also mean any building, especially one of a large and public character, such as a palace or. mansion; and hence some contend that it should be interpreted here of 'the silkworm house.' We are to conceive of the lady, after, having gathered the materials for sacrificial use, then preparing them according to rule, and while it is yet dark on the morning of the -sacrificial day, going with them into the temple, and setting them forth in their proper vessels and places.

With head-dress reverently rising aloft, Early, while yet it is night, she is in the prince's (temple). In her head-dress, slowly retiring, She returns (to her own apartments).

ODE 4. THE ZHÂI PIN.

CELEBRATING THE DILIGENCE AND REVERENCE OF THE YOUNG WIFE OF AN OFFICER, DOING HER PART IN SACRIFICIAL OFFERINGS.

She gathers the large duckweed, By the banks of the stream in the southern valley. She gathers the pondweed, In those pools left by the floods.

She deposits what she gathers, In her square baskets and round ones. She boils it, In her tripods and pans.

She sets forth her preparations, Under the window in the ancestral chamber[1]. Who superintends the business? It is (this) reverent young lady.

1. 'The ancestral chamber' was a room behind the temple of the family, dedicated specially to the ancestor of the officer whose wife is the subject of the piece. The princes of states were succeeded, as a rule, by the eldest son of the wife proper. Their sons by other wives were called 'other sons.' The eldest son by the wife proper of one of them became the 'great ancestor' of the clan descended from him, and 'the ancestral chamber' was an apartment dedicated to him. Mâo and other interpreters, going on certain statements as to the training of daughters in the business of sacrificing in this apartment for three months previous to their marriage, contend that the lady spoken of here was not yet married, but was only undergoing this preparatory education. It is not necessary, however, to adopt this interpretation. The lady appears doing the same duties as the wife in the former piece.

BOOK III. THE ODES OF PHEI.

WHEN king Wû overthrew the dynasty of Shang, the domain of its kings was divided into three portions, the northern portion being called Phei, the southern Yung, and the eastern Wei, the rulers of which last in course of time absorbed the other two. It is impossible to say why the old names were retained in the arrangement of the odes in this Part of the Shih, for it is acknowledged on all hands that the pieces in Books iii and iv, as well as those of Book v, are all odes of Wei.

ODE 4. THE ZAH YÜEH.

SUPPOSED TO BE THE COMPLAINT AND APPEAL OF KWANG KIANG, A MARCHIONESS OF WEI, AGAINST THE BAD TREATMENT SHE RECEIVED FROM HER HUSBAND.

All the Chinese critics give this interpretation of the piece. Kwang Kiang was a daughter of the house of Khî, about the middle of the eighth century B.C., and was married to the marquis Yang, known in history as 'duke Kwang,' of Wei. She was a lady of admirable character, and beautiful; but her husband proved faithless and unkind. In this ode she makes her subdued moan, appealing to the sun and moon, as if they could take cognizance of the way in which she was treated. Possibly, however, the addressing those bodies may simply be an instance of prosopopoeia.

O sun, O moon, Which enlighten this lower earth! Here is this man, Who treats me not according to the ancient rule. How can he get his mind settled? Would he then not regard me?

O sun, O moon, Which overshadow this lower earth! Here is this man, Who will not be friendly with me. How can he get his mind settled? Would he then not respond to me?

O sun, O moon, Which come forth from the east! Here is this man, With virtuous words, but really not good. How can he get his mind settled? Would he then allow me to be forgotten?

O sun, O moon, From the east that come forth! O father, O mother, There is no sequel to your nourishing of me. How can he get his mind settled? Would he then respond tome contrary to all reason?

ODE 15, STANZA 1. THE PEI MAN.

AN OFFICER OF WEI SETS FORTH HIS HARD LOT, THROUGH DISTRESSES AND THE BURDENS LAID UPON HIM, AND HIS SILENCE UNDER IT IN SUBMISSION TO HEAVEN.

I go out at the north gate, With my heart full of sorrow. Straitened am I and poor, And no one takes knowledge of my distress. So it is! Heaven has done it[1];—What then shall I say?

BOOK IV. THE ODES OF YUNG.

See the preliminary note on p. 433.

ODE 1. THE PAI KÂU.

PROTEST OF A WIDOW AGAINST BEING URGED TO MARRY AGAIN, AND HER APPEAL TO HER MOTHER AND TO HEAVEN.

THIS piece, it is said, was made by Kung Kiang, the widow of Kung-po, son of the marquis Hsî Of Wei (B.C. 855-814). Kung-po having died an early death, her parents (who must have been the marquis of Khî and his wife or one of the ladies of his harem) wanted to force her to a second marriage, against which she protests. The ode was preserved, no doubt, as an example of

1. The 'Complete Digest of Comments on the Shih' warns its readers not to take 'Heaven' here as synonymous with Ming, 'what is decreed or Commanded.' The writer does not go on to define the precise idea which he understood the character to convey. This appears to be what we often mean by 'Providence,' when we speak of anything permitted, rather than appointed, by the supreme ruling Power.

what the Chinese have always considered a great virtue,—the refusal of a, widow to marry again.

It floats about, that boat of cypress wood, There in the middle of the Ho [1]. With his two tufts of hair falling over his forehead [2], He was my mate; And I swear that till death I will have no other. O mother, O Heavens[3], Why will you not understand me?

It floats about, that boat of cypress wood, There by the side of the Ho. With his two tufts of hair falling over his forehead, He was my only one; And I swear that till death I will not do the evil thing. O mother, O Heaven, Why will you not understand me?

ODE 3, STANZA 2. THE KÜN-DZE KIEH LÂO.

CONTRAST BETWEEN THE BEAUTY AND SPLENDOUR OF HSÜAN KIANG AND HER VICIOUSNESS.

Hsüan Kiang was a princess of Khî, Who, towards the close of the seventh century B.C., became wife to the marquis of Wei, known as duke Hsüan. She was beautiful and unfortunate, but various things are related of her indicative of the grossest immoralities prevailing in the court of Wei.

How rich and splendid Is her pheasant-figured

1. These allusive lines, probably, indicate the speaker's widowhood, Which left her like 'a boat floating about on the water.'
2. Such was the mode in which the hair was kept, while a boy or young man's parents were alive, parted into two tufts from the pia mater, and brought down as low as the eyebrows on either side of the forehead.
3. Mâo, thought that the lady intended her father by 'Heaven;' while Kû held that her father may have been dead, and that the mother is called Heaven, with reference to the kindness and protection that she ought to show. There seems rather to be in the term a wild, and not very intelligent, appeal to the supreme Power in heaven.

robe[1]! Her black hair in masses like clouds, No false locks does she descend to. There are her earplugs of jade, Her comb-pin of ivory, And her high forehead, so white. She appears like a visitant from heaven! She appears like a goddess[2].

ODE 6, STANZAS 1 AND 2. THE TING KIH FANG KÛNG.

CELEBRATING THE PRAISE OF DUKE WIN;—HIS DILIGENCE, FORESIGHT, USE OF DIVINATION, AND OTHER QUALITIES.

The state of Wei was reduced to extremity by an irruption of some northern hordes in B.C. 660, and had nearly disappeared from among the states of Kau. Under the marquis Wei, known in history as duke Wan, its fortunes revived, and he became a sort of second founder of the state.

When Ting culminated (at night-fall)[3] He began to build the palace at Khû [4], Determining

1. The lady is introduced arrayed in the gorgeous robes worn by the princess of a state in the ancestral temple.
2. P. Lacharme translated these two concluding lines by 'Tu primo aspectu coelos (pulchritudine), et imperatorem (majestate) adaequas,' without any sanction of the Chinese critics; and moreover there was no Tî (###) in the sense of imperator then in China. The sovereigns of Kau were Wang or kings. Kû Hsî expands the lines thus:—'Such is the beauty of her robes and appearance, that beholders are struck with awe, as if she were a spiritual being.' Hsü Khien (Yüan dynasty) deals with them thus:—With such splendour of beauty and dress, how is it that she is here? She has come down from heaven I She is a spiritual being!'
3. Ting is the name of a small space in the heavens, embracing *alpha* Markab and another star of Pegasus. Its culminating at night-fall was the signal that the labours of husbandry were over for the year, and that building operations should be taken in hand. Great as was the urgency for the building of his new capital, duke Win would not take it in hand till the proper time for such a labour was arrived.
4. Khû, or Khû-khiû, was the new capital of Wei, in the present district of Khang-wû, department Zhâo-kâu, Shan-tung.

its aspects by means of the sun. He built the palace at Khû. He planted about it hazel and chestnut trees, The Î, the Thung, the Dze, and the varnish tree. Which, when cut down, might afford materials for lutes.

He ascended those old walls, And thence surveyed (the site of) Khû. He surveyed Khû and Thang[1], With the lofty hills and high elevations about. He descended and examined the mulberry trees. He then divined by the tortoise-shell, and got a favourable response [2]; And thus the issue has been truly good.

BOOK V. THE ODES OF WEI.

IT has been said on the title of Book iii, that Wei at first was the eastern portion of the old domain of the kings of Shang. With this a brother of king Wû, called Khang-shû, was invested. The principality was afterwards increased by the absorption of Phei and Yung. It came to embrace portions of the present provinces of Kih-lî, Shan-tung, and Ho-nan. It outlasted the dynasty of Kâu itself, the last prince of Wei being reduced to the ranks of the people only during the dynasty of Khin.

ODE 4, STANZAS I AND 2. THE MANG.

AN UNFORTUNATE WOMAN, WHO HAD BEEN SEDUCED INTO AN IMPROPER CONNEXION, NOW CAST OFF, RELATES AND BEMOANS HER SAD CASE.

An extract is given from the pathetic history here related, because it shows how divination was used among the common people, and entered generally into the ordinary affairs of life.

A simple-looking lad you were, Carrying cloth

1. Thang was the name of a town, evidently not far from Khû.
2. We have seen before how divination was resorted to on occasion of new undertakings, especially in proceeding to rear a city.

to exchange it for silk. (But) you came not so to purchase silk;—You came to make proposals to me. I convoyed you through the Khî [1], As far as Tun-khiû [2], 'It is not I,' (I said), 'who would protract the time; But you have had no good go-between. I pray you be not angry, And let autumn be the time.'

I ascended that ruinous wall, To look towards Fû-kwan [3]; And when I saw (you) not (coming from) it, My tears flowed in streams. When I did see (you coming from) Fû-kwan, I laughed and I spoke. You had consulted, (you said), the tortoiseshell and the divining stalks, And there was nothing unfavourable in their response [4]. 'Then come,' (I said), 'with your carriage, And I will remove with my goods.'

BOOK VI. THE ODES OF THE ROYAL DOMAIN.

KING Wan, it has been seen, had for his capital the city of Fang, from which his son, king Wû, moved the seat of government to Hâo. In the time of king Khang, a city was built by the duke

1. The Khî was a famous river of Wei.
2. Tun-khiû was a well-known place—'the mound or height of Tun'-south of the Wei.
3. 'Fû-kwan must have been the place where the man lived, according to Kû. Rather, it must have been a pass (Fû-kwan may mean 'the gate or pass of Fû'), through which he would come, and was visible from near the residence of the woman.
4 Ying tâ observes that the man had never divined about the matter, and said that he had done so only to complete the process of seduction. The critics dwell on the inconsistency of divination being resorted to in such a case:—'Divination is proper only if used in reference to what is right and moral.'

of Kâu, near the present Lo-yang, and called 'the eastern capital.' Meetings of the princes of the states assembled there; but the court continued to be held at Hâo till the accession of king Phing in B.C. 770. From that time, the kings of Kâu sank nearly to the level of the princes of the states, and the poems collected in their domain were classed among the 'Lessons of Manners from the States,' though still distinguished by the epithet 'royal' prefixed to them.

ODE 1, STANZA 1. THE SHÛ-LÎ.

AN OFFICER DESCRIBES HIS MELANCHOLY AND REFLECTIONS ON SEEING THE DESOLATION OF THE OLD CAPITAL OF KAU, MAKING HIS MOAN TO HEAVEN BECAUSE OF IT.

There is no specific mention of the old. capital of Kâu in the piece, but the schools of Mâo and Kû are agreed in this interpretation, which is much more likely than any of the others that have been proposed.

There was the millet with its drooping heads; There was the sacrificial millet coming into blade[1]. Slowly I moved about, In my heart all-agitated. Those who knew me said I was sad at heart. Those who did not know me, Said I was seeking for something.

O thou distant and azure Heaven[2]! By what man was this (brought about)[3]?

1. That is, there where the ancestral temple and other grand buildings of Hâo had once stood.
2. 'He cried out to Heaven,' says Yen Zhan, 'and told (his distress), but he calls it distant in its azure brightness, lamenting that his complaint was not heard.' This is, probably, the correct explanation of the language. The speaker would by it express his grief that the dynasty of Kâu and its people were abandoned and uncared for by Heaven.
3. Referring to king Yû, whose reckless course had led to the destruction of Hâo by the Zung, and in a minor degree to his son, king Phing, who had subsequently removed to the eastern capital.

ODE 9, STANZAS 1 AND 3. THE TÂ KÜ.

A LADY EXCUSES HERSELF FOR NOT FLYING TO HER LOVER BY HER FEAR OF A SEVERE AND VIRTUOUS MAGISTRATE, AND SWEARS TO HIS THAT SHE IS SINCERE IN HER ATTACHMENT TO HIM.

His great carriage rolls along, And his robes of rank glitter like the young sedge. Do I not think of you? But I am afraid of this officer, and dare not (fly to you).

While living we may have to occupy different apartments; But, when dead, we shall share the same grave. If you say that I am not sincere, By the bright sun I swear that I am[1].

BOOK X. THE, ODES OF THANG.

THE odes of Thang were really the odes of Zin, the greatest of the fiefs of Kâu until the rise of Khin. King Khang, in B.C. 1107, invested his younger brother, called Shû-yü, with the territory where Yâo was supposed to have ruled anciently as the marquis of Thang, in the present department of Thâi-yüan, Shan-hsî, the fief retaining that ancient name. Subsequently the name of the state was changed to Zin, from the river Zin in the southern part of it.

ODE, 8, STANZA 1. THE PÂO YÜ.

THE MEN OF ZIN, CALLED OUT TO WARFARE BY THE KING'S ORDER, MOURN OVER THE CONSEQUENT SUFFERING OF THEIR PARENTS, AND LONG FOR THEIR RETURN TO THEIR ORDINARY AGRICULTURAL PURSUITS, MAKING THEIR APPEAL TO HEAVEN.

Sû-sû go the feathers of the wild geese, As

1. In the 'Complete Digest' this oath is expanded in the following way:—'These words are from my heart. If you think that they are not sincere, there is (a Power) above, like the bright sun, observing me;—how should my words not be sincere?'

they settle on the bushy oaks[1]. The king's affairs must not be slackly discharged, And (so) we cannot plant our millets;—What will our parents have to rely on? O thou distant and azure Heaven [2]! When shall we be in our places again?

ODE 11. THE KO SHANG.

A WIFE MOURNS THE DEATH OF HER HUSBAND, REFUSING TO BE COMFORTED, AND DECLARES THAT SHE WILL CHERISH HIS MEMORY TILL HER OWN DEATH.

It is supposed that the husband whose death is bewailed in this piece had died in one of the military expeditions of which duke Hsien (B.C. 676-651) was fond. It may have been so, but there is nothing in the piece to make us think of duke Hsien. I give it a place in the volume, not because of the religious sentiment in it, but because of the absence of that sentiment, Where we might expect it. The lady shows the grand virtue of a Chinese widow, in that she will never marry again. And her grief would not be assuaged. The days would all seem long summer days, and the nights all long winter nights; so that a hundred long years would seem to drag their slow course, But there is not any hope expressed of a re-union with her husband in another state. The 'abode' and the 'chamber' of which she speaks are to be understood of his grave; and her thoughts do not appear to go beyond it.

The dolichos grows, covering the thorn trees; The convolvulus spreads all over the waste [3]. The

1. Trees are not the proper. place for geese to rest on; and the attempt to do so is productive of much noise and trouble to the birds. The lines would seem to allude to the hardships of the soldiers' lot, called from their homes to go on a distant expedition.
2. See note 2 on ode I of Book vi, where Heaven is appealed to in the same language.
3. These two lines are taken as allusive, the speaker being led by the sight of the weak plants supported by the trees, shrubs, and tombs, to think of her own desolate, unsupported condition. But they may also be taken as narrative, and descriptive of the battleground, where her husband had met his death.

man of my admiration is no more here;—With whom can I dwell? I abide alone.

The dolichos grows, covering the jujube trees; The convolvulus spreads all over the tombs. The man of my admiration is no more here;—With whom can I dwell? I rest alone.

How beautiful was the pillow of horn! How splendid was the embroidered coverlet[1]! The man of my admiration is no more here;—With whom can I dwell? Alone (I wait for) the morning.

Through the (long) days of summer, Through the (long) nights of winter (shall I be alone), Till the lapse of a hundred years, When I shall go home to his abode.

Through the (long) nights of winter, Through the (long) days of summer(shall I be alone), Till the lapse of a hundred years, When I shall go home to his chamber.

BOOK XI. THE ODES OF KHIN.

THE state of Khin took its name from its earliest principal city, in the present district of Khing-shui, in Khin Kau, Kan-sû. Its chiefs claimed to be descended from Yî, who appears in the Shû as the forester of Shun, and the assistant of the great Yü in his labours on the flood of Yâo. The history of his descendants is very imperfectly related till we come to a Fei-Dze, who had charge of the herds of horses belonging to king Hsiâo (B.C. 90989.5), and in consequence of his good services, was invested with

1. These things had been ornaments of the bridal chamber; and as the widow thinks of them, her grief becomes more intense.

the small territory of Khin, as an attached state. A descendant of his, known as duke Hsiang, in consequence of his loyal services, when the capital was moved to the east in B.C. 770, was raised to the dignity of an earl, and took his place among the great feudal princes of the kingdom, receiving also a large portion of territory, which included the ancient capital of the House of Kâu. In course of time Khin, as is well known, superseded the dynasty of Kâu, having gradually moved its capital more and more to the east. The people of Khin were, no doubt, mainly composed of the wild tribes of the west.

ODE 6, STANZA 1. THE HWANG NIÂO.

LAMENT FOR THREE WORTHIES OF KHIN, WHO WERE BURIED IN THE SAME GRAVE WITH DUKE MÛ.

There is no difficulty or difference in the interpretation of this piece; and it brings us down to B.C. 621. Then died duke Mû, after playing an important part in the north-west of China for thirty-nine years. The Zo Kwan, under the sixth year of duke Wan, makes mention of Mû's requiring that the three brothers here celebrated should be buried with him, and of the composition of this piece in consequence. Sze-mâ Khien says that this barbarous practice began with Mû's predecessor, with whom sixty-six persons were buried alive, and that one hundred and seventy-seven in all were buried with Mû. The death of the last distinguished man of the House of Khin, the emperor [1], was subsequently celebrated by the entombment with him of all the inmates of his harem.

They flit about, the yellow birds, And rest upon the jujube trees [1]. Who followed duke Mû in the grave? Dze-kü Yen-hsî. And this Yen-hsî Was a man above a hundred. When he came to the

1. It is difficult to see the relation between these two allusive lines and the rest of the stanza. Some say that it is this,-that the people loved the three victims as they liked the birds; others that the birds among the trees were in their proper place,—very different from the brothers in the grave of duke Mû.

grave, He looked terrified and trembled. Thou azure Heaven there! Could he have been redeemed, We would have given a hundred (ordinary) men for him[1].

BOOK XV. THE ODES OF PIN.

DUKE Liû, an ancestor of the Kâu family, made a settlement, according to its traditions, in B.C. 1797, in Pin, the site of which is pointed out, 90 lî to the west of the present district city of San-shui, in Pin Kau, Shen-hsî, where the tribe remained till the movement eastwards of Than-fû, celebrated in the first decade of the Major Odes of the Kingdom, ode 3. The duke of Kâu, during the minority of king Khang, made, it is supposed, the first of the pieces in this Book, describing for the instruction of the young monarch, the ancient ways of their fathers in Pin; and subsequently some one compiled other, odes made by the duke, and others also about him, and brought them together under the common name of 'the Odes of Pin.'

ODE 1, STANZA 8. THE KHÎ YÜEH.

DESCRIBING LIFE IN PIN IN THE OLDEN TIME; THE PROVIDENT ARRANGEMENTS THERE TO SECURE THE CONSTANT SUPPLY OF FOOD AND RAIMENT,— WHATEVER WAS NECESSARY FOR THE SUPPORT AND COMFORT OF THE PEOPLE.

If the piece was made, as the Chinese critics all suppose, by the duke of Kâu, we must still suppose that he writes in the person of an old farmer or yeoman of Pin. The picture which it gives of the manners of the Chinese people, their thrifty, provident ways, their agriculture and weaving, nearly 3,700 years ago, is

1. This appeal to Heaven is like what we met with in the first of the Odes of the Royal Domain, and the eighth of those of Thang.

full of interest; but it is not till we come to the concluding stanza that we find anything bearing on their religious practices

In the days of (our) second month, they hew out the ice with harmonious blows [1]; And in those of (our) third month, they convey it to the ice-houses, (Which they open) in those of (our) fourth, early in the morning A lamb having been offered in sacrifice with scallions[2]. In the ninth month, it is cold, with frost. In the tenth month, they sweep clean their stack-sites. (Taking) the two bottles of spirits to be offered to their ruler, And having killed their lambs and sheep, They go to his hall, And raising

1. They went for the ice to the deep recesses of the hills, and wherever it was to be found in the best condition.
2.. It is said in the last chapter of 'the Great Learning,' that 'the family which keeps its stores of ice does not rear cattle or sheep,' meaning that the possessor of an ice-house must be supposed to be very wealthy, and above the necessity of increasing his means in the way described. Probably, the having ice-houses by high ministers and heads of clans was an innovation on the earlier custom, according to which such a distinction was proper only to the king, or the princes of states, on whom it devolved as I the fathers of the people,' to impart from their stores in the hot season as might be necessary. The third and fourth lines of this stanza are to be understood of what was done by the orders of the ruler of the tribe of Kâu in Pin. In the Official Book of Kâu, Part 1, ch. 5, we have a description of the duties of 'the Providers of Ice,' and the same subject is treated in the sixth Book of 'the Record of Rites,' sections 2 and 6. The ice having been collected and stored in winter, the ice-houses were solemnly opened in the spring. A sacrifice was offered to 'the Ruler of Cold, the Spirit of the Ice' and of the first ice brought forth an offering was set out in the apartment behind the principal hall of the ancestral temple. A sacrifice to the same Ruler of Cold, it is said, had also been offered when the ice began to be collected. The ceremony may be taken as an illustration of the manner in which religious services entered into the life of the ancient Chinese.

the cup of rhinoceros horn, Wish him long life,—that he may live for ever[1].

1. The custom described in the five concluding lines is mentioned to show the good and loyal feeling of the people of Pin towards their chief Having finished all the agricultural labours of the year, and being now prepared to enjoy the results of their industry, the first thing they do is to hasten to the hall of their ruler, and ask him to share in their joy, and express their loyal wishes for his happiness.

BIBLIOBAZAAR

The essential book market!

Did you know that you can get any of our titles in large print?

Did you know that we have an ever-growing collection of books in many languages?

**Order online:
www.bibliobazaar.com**

Find all of your favorite classic books!

Stay up to date with the latest government reports!

At BiblioBazaar, we aim to make knowledge more accessible by making thousands of titles available to you- *quickly and affordably*.

Contact us:
BiblioBazaar
PO Box 21206
Charleston, SC 29413

Printed in Great Britain
by Amazon